NEW DIRECTIONS FOR CHILD A[

William Damon, *Stanford University*
EDITOR-IN-CHIEF

# Homeless and Working Youth Around the World: Exploring Developmental Issues

Marcela Raffaelli
*University of Nebraska*

Reed W. Larson
*University of Illinois*

EDITORS

Number 85, Fall 1999

JOSSEY-BASS PUBLISHERS
San Francisco

HOMELESS AND WORKING YOUTH AROUND THE WORLD: EXPLORING
DEVELOPMENTAL ISSUES
*Marcela Raffaelli, Reed W. Larson* (eds.)
New Directions for Child and Adolescent Development, no. 85
*William Damon*, Editor-in-Chief

Microfilm copies of issues and articles are available in 16mm and 35mm,
as well as microfiche in 105mm, through University Microfilms Inc., 300
North Zeeb Road, Ann Arbor, Michigan 48106–1346.

ISSN 1520-3247       ISBN 0-7879-1252-2

NEW DIRECTIONS FOR CHILD AND ADOLESCENT DEVELOPMENT is part of
The Jossey-Bass Education Series and is published quarterly by Jossey-
Bass Inc., Publishers, 350 Sansome Street, San Francisco, California
94104–1342. Periodicals postage paid at San Francisco, California, and at
additional mailing offices. Postmaster: Send address changes to New
Directions for Child and Adolescent Development, Jossey-Bass Inc., Publishers, 350 Sansome Street, San Francisco, California 94104–1342.

*New Directions for Child and Adolescent Development* is indexed in Bio-
sciences Information Service, Current Index to Journals in Education
(ERIC), Psychological Abstracts, and Sociological Abstracts.

SUBSCRIPTIONS cost $67.00 for individuals and $115.00 for institutions,
agencies, and libraries.

EDITORIAL CORRESPONDENCE should be sent to the Editor-in-Chief,
William Damon, Stanford Center on Adolescence, Cypress Building C,
Stanford University, Stanford, California 94305–4145.

Cover photograph by Wernher Krutein/PHOTOVAULT © 1990.

Jossey-Bass Web address: www.josseybass.com

Printed in the United States of America on acid-free recycled paper containing 100 percent recovered waste paper, of which at least 20 percent is
postconsumer waste.

# CONTENTS

# Editors' Notes

This volume focuses on developmental issues among street youth. The term *street youth*, or *street children*, is deceptively simple and conceals enormous variation in the experiences of youngsters who share the common condition of being "out of place" in street environments, spending their lives largely outside the spheres typically considered appropriate for children, such as home, school, and recreational settings (Connolly and Ennew, 1996). The United Nations defines a street child as "any boy or girl . . . for whom the street (in the widest sense of the word, including unoccupied dwellings, wasteland, etc.) has become his or her habitual abode and/or source of livelihood; and who is inadequately protected, supervised, or directed by responsible adults" (quoted in Lusk, 1992, p. 294). This broad definition encompasses several subgroups of street youth, including youngsters who work and sometimes live on city streets in developing countries as well as the runaway, homeless, and throw-away adolescents found in developed nations.

The number of street youth worldwide is hotly debated, with estimates ranging from several million to over 100 million (UNICEF, 1989, 1993). This lack of consensus results in part from lack of reliable data and in part from definitional confusion over who street youth are (Hutz, Bandeira, Koller, and Forster, 1997). Evidence of the magnitude of the street youth population can be found on city streets all over the world, ranging from the street vendor selling newspapers and candy at a traffic light in Mexico City to the runaway teen begging outside a New York City subway station to the groups of children who surround tourists in Abidjan asking for a *cadeau* (present).

In addition to being excluded from society's institutions, street youth have been excluded from the realm of developmental research. Little is known about the developmental trajectories of street youth, and virtually no research on street youth has appeared in mainstream developmental journals. Instead, most street youth research has been published in journals devoted to social work, education, health, anthropology, and cross-cultural psychology (see Connolly and Ennew, 1996). The goal of this volume is to begin exploring developmental issues among street youth from around the world and to familiarize developmental researchers with this population.

## Why Should Developmentalists Study Street Youth?

The neglect of street youth by developmental scholars represents a loss not only to the field of street youth research but also to the discipline of human development. Homeless and working street youth face tremendous challenges in their daily lives, and high-quality research is needed to inform interventions, guide social policy, and provide information for service providers and street youth workers attempting to help them face these challenges. Unless

New Directions for Child and Adolescent Development, no. 85, Fall 1999 © Jossey-Bass Publishers    1 researchers studying street youth have a developmental perspective, they may obtain an inaccurate picture of the age-related capabilities and vulnerabilities of these youth and the trajectories these youth are on. Developmental research, with its explicit focus on change and adjustment across time, has the potential to illuminate the adaptation processes of street youth and the long-term impact of street life.

Research on street youth can also provide direct benefits to developmental science, by expanding our understanding of basic developmental processes. Because street youth grow up in circumstances that violate fundamental assumptions about what is needed for healthy development to occur, studying them can enhance our understanding of development in a number of ways. On the theoretical level, the study of street youth can enable scholars to evaluate the extent to which specific developmental processes vary under differing environmental circumstances. Indeed, research on mathematical reasoning among child vendors has yielded unique information about the impact of context on the development of computational skills (Carraher, Carraher, and Schliemann, 1985). The study of homeless and working street children could also contribute to the growing literature on developmental risk and resilience. Resilience researchers have learned to take advantage of natural experiments, however unfortunate, that impose a variety of stressors on children, such as war, natural disasters, or abusive situations (Masten, 1994). Street youth can provide a unique source of information because these youngsters are growing up in situations that typically impose extreme, chronic, and often uncontrollable demands for coping and adjustment. Finally, on a more pragmatic level, as Western developmental psychologists begin forming linkages with international colleagues, they need to be aware that poverty and deprivation are common experiences in the lives of many of the world's children and that the white, European, middle-class families on which much developmental research and theory has focused characterizes a minority of the world's population.

## Organization of This Volume

To convey the diversity of the world's street youth, this volume of *New Directions for Child Development* takes a geographical approach, presenting work from four different regions (India, South America, Africa, and North America). Although street children are found in virtually every country around the world and can be considered a "universal" phenomenon, different factors have been linked to their presence in specific geographical regions. For example, in India and most of Latin America, poverty is a major force leading children to the streets, whereas in the United States, the majority of youngsters found on city streets appear to be escaping dysfunctional families. In Africa, where poverty and civil unrest were once the main factors in forcing children out of their homes, the AIDS epidemic has now become a key factor in the phenomenon of street youth (Rutayuga, 1992).

In addition to variations in the factors that contribute to the street youth population, there is a great deal of diversity in the social, cultural, and historical backgrounds of regions of the world where street children are found, resulting in large differences in the experiences of these youngsters. For example, in India, which is predominantly Hindu, working street youth occupy a position in the social order that has been accepted for centuries (see Chapter One), whereas in Brazil, child labor laws and a Catholic cultural tradition have created a more oppositional relationship between street youth and the rest of society (see Chapter Two).

To provide readers with an understanding of these contextual variations, each author was asked to begin with a brief description of the cultural, historical, and economic factors that shape the lives of street youth in the region. We regard this background as essential to providing the context for interpreting specific research findings. In the body of each chapter, authors then delve into a set of developmental questions and findings of their own choosing. These reflect issues relevant to the population they are focusing on, as well as the unique interests and methodologies of the authors. We hope that as a whole the chapters convey a flavor of the developmental issues relevant to street youth around the world.

In Chapter One, Suman Verma describes the condition of working street youth in India, giving particular attention to her novel research findings on the daily activities of these youngsters. Her data, from a sample of working street youth who return to their families in the evening, suggest not only the normality of their lives—they work, interact with peers, and have largely positive relationships with their parents—but also how the absence of schooling and various sources of chronic stress impair their life chances and their ability to develop advanced adjustment skills.

In Chapter Two, Marcelo Diversi, Ney Moraes filho, and Margareth Morelli report on Diversi's ethnographic study of homeless street youth in Campinas, Brazil. Drawing on spontaneous stories told by homeless youngsters, their account reveals that these youth, far from being victims, are active interpreters and creators of their own lives. At the same time, it is evident that these youth face enormous challenges in their day-to-day lives and that their developing identities are affected and skewed by a dominant public perception of them as parasites and criminals.

In Chapter Three, Lewis Aptekar and Lynda M. Ciano-Federoff report on a study of street youth in Kenya that employed both quantitative and qualitative data to examine gender differences in the psychological adjustment of these young people. The comparison reveals that for male street youth in Kenya, leaving an impoverished family situation is a culturally appropriate way of coping with the demands of poverty and the first step toward independence and maturity. In contrast, because girls are traditionally expected to remain in the home, their presence on the street is the result of family breakdown or individual distress and appears to lead to more negative developmental outcomes.

Jacqueline Smollar examines the developmental circumstances of street youth in North America in Chapter Four. She reviews the changing population of homeless youth in the United States and then assesses the extent to which life on the street affects the four individual characteristics that have been linked to positive adolescent development: a sense of industry and competency, a feeling of connectedness to others and to society, a sense of control over one's fate in life, and a stable sense of identity.

In Chapter Five, Claudio S. Hutz and Sílvia H. Koller present a condensed handbook for carrying out research on street youth. They draw on their experience as the founders of a university-based research center to develop a set of guidelines for street youth researchers, particularly those attempting to do quantitative research. They also discuss the ethical implications of conducting research with homeless and working street youth.

We are especially pleased that the volume concludes with a commentary by Felton Earls and Maya Carlson. A pediatrician and a psychologist, respectively, they provide a model that synthesizes concerns across disciplines including medicine and public health and bring a human rights perspective to the study of impoverished youth.

Marcela Raffaelli
Reed W. Larson
Editors

## References

Carraher, T., Carraher, S., and Schliemann, A. "Mathematics in the Streets and Schools." *British Journal of Developmental Psychology,* 1985, *3,* 21–29.

Connolly, M., and Ennew, J. "Introduction: Children out of Place." *Childhood,* 1996, *3,* 131–145.

Hutz, C. S., Bandeira, D. R., Koller, S. H., and Forster, L. K. "Who Are Brazilian Street Children?" Unpublished manuscript, Universidade Federal do Rio Grande do Sul, Porto Alegre, Brazil, 1997.

Lusk, M. W. "Street Children of Rio de Janeiro." *International Social Work,* 1992, *35,* 293–305.

Masten, A. S. "Resilience in Individual Development: Successful Adaptation Despite Risk and Adversity." In M. C. Wang and E. W. Gordon (eds.), *Educational Resilience in Inner-City America: Challenges and Prospects.* Mahwah, N.J.: Erlbaum, 1994.

Rutayuga, J.B.K. "Assistance to AIDS Orphans Within the Family/Kinship System and Local Institutions: A Program for East Africa." *AIDS Education and Prevention,* 1992, 57(Supp.), 57–68.

UNICEF. *The State of the World's Children.* Oxford: Oxford University Press, 1989.

UNICEF. *The State of the World's Children.* Oxford: Oxford University Press, 1993.

MARCELA RAFFAELLI *is an assistant professor with a joint appointment in the Department of Psychology and the Institute for Ethnic Studies at the University of Nebraska-Lincoln.*

REED W. LARSON *is a professor in the Departments of Human and Community Development, Psychology, Kinesiology, and Leisure Studies at the University of Illinois in Urbana-Champaign.*

*Life on the streets is hazardous for Indian street children and provides limited opportunities for the development of cognitive skills that would give them entree into middle-class life. Nonetheless, these youth learn many useful life skills for survival and coping in crisis.*

# Socialization for Survival: Developmental Issues Among Working Street Children in India

*Suman Verma*

"The taxi stopped at a red light on the Bandra flyover," writes Mira Nair, sharing the first image that inspired her remarkable film *Salaam Bombay:*

> Within moments I was surrounded by street children of all ages performing, begging, blowing soap-bubbles, dancing, washing windows with a dirty rag—anything for a few paise. In the centre of the intersection I could see a fifteen-year-old boy, his torso rising from maimed legs that rested on a wooden platform on wheels pushing himself by his hands from car to car, his skinny fingers stretching into each car window, begging. The light changed to green. I was terrified of what might happen to him now, surrounded as he was by trucks, cars, scooters, rickshaws. The boy caught hold of the back of the scooter, carried himself along at top speed until he reached the edge of the road, and there, propelled by sheer momentum, pirouetted flamboyantly, his hands raised skywards, saluting the deafening applause of an imaginary audience [Nair and Taraporevala, 1989, p. 3].

Despite his handicap, this child demonstrates remarkable survival instincts and courage in his daily struggle with the virulent environment of city streets—while making a living. He is, at once, at extreme developmental risk and remarkably competent.

This chapter explores these two competing sentiments in Nair's reaction. I examine the hazards of the lives of Indian working street children and the ways in which their daily contexts limit their development. I also ask, what

New Directions for Child and Adolescent Development, no. 85, Fall 1999 © Jossey-Bass Publishers competencies do street children develop in this environment? My focus is on describing the social settings in which these children participate and what they learn from each of these settings. How do the on-the-street work context, peer group, community, and family operate to structure street children's experiences? How are these youth influenced by the street settings they encounter, and how do they make use of them?

My theoretical orientation is ecological, focusing on environmental influences ranging from the family to societal values (Kagitçibasi, 1996). What I wish to communicate is that street children encounter a different environment and have a different set of learning experiences, compared to their counterparts from the larger society. The situational demands of street life in turn necessitate development of a very different set of skills—in order to increase their chances of survival. In Lewinian terms, all behavior must be understood in light of the field that provides the context for that behavior. Children's interactions in daily behavior settings shape not only their economic activities and lifestyles but also their socialization, interpersonal relationships, and general cognitive and perceptual functioning and development (Sinha, 1982). We can expect that street children will be socialized to learn the roles, competencies, and adaptive skills essential to survive competently on the streets. In this chapter, I consider skills ranging from those needed for self-preservation and economic survival to more fundamental interpersonal and cognitive ones.

The first section of the chapter presents a general description of the situation of street children in India. After that I describe my research on the different social contexts that make up their daily lives. Next I examine how the daily experiences of street children, particularly with their families, provide a context for development of certain skills but not others. In the last section I put forward proposals for future research and action to deal with children living in these stressful life conditions.

## Street Children in India

Street children in India must be understood in terms of the larger category of working children.

**The Working Child: A Historical Overview.** Child work has existed throughout recorded Indian history, and this legacy, reflected in Hindu mythology, legends, and classical literature, influences current attitudes toward the roles of children (Dube, 1981). In the Hindu epics, education was imparted by a guru (sage) in his hermitage, and students participated in the domestic chores of the guru's household. Among agriculturists, children had specific tasks, such as cattle grazing and keeping a watch on crops to frighten away birds and beasts. Among artisans, training in the craft started early, and by the teen years children were contributing substantially to the economic activities of both the family and the community. Dube (1981, p. 184) adds that "children were entrusted with work that was time consuming but not arduous, they could combine recreation with work, work was never disassociated from play and education." However, because children's activities were enmeshed with the activities of adults, the constraints, limitations, and deprivations of a particular group also characterized the life of its children. References to slavery, domestic service, and master-servant relationships in literature, particularly Buddhist literature, unmistakably point toward the presence of children toiling as slaves and servants at the mercy of their masters. Thus with the advent of urbanization and industrialization, children became involved in jobs outside the home carried out under conditions of exploitation that were monotonous, strenuous, and unduly prolonged and that interfered with schooling, recreation, and general well-being (Mendelievich, 1980).

In India today children work as main and marginal workers, in both the organized and unorganized sectors in rural and urban economies. They can be found working in major industries such as gem polishing, glass manufacturing, and carpet weaving; as bonded laborers (children given in settlement of debts); as part of family labor in all the contexts of agriculture, industry, and home-based work; and as street children working in the service sector of semi-urban and urban India. These are nonexclusive categories and often overlap (Burra, 1997). This chapter focuses exclusively on the state of the street child worker in India; Burra (1997) and Weiner (1991) provide thoughtful discussions on the conditions of children working in the organized sectors in India.

**Realities of the Child Street Worker.** Street children in India can be seen working, living, or just hanging around in streets, market areas, intersections, parking areas, and railway stations. They are engaged in a host of remunerative activities including ragpicking, vending, selling newspapers, cleaning cars, begging, shining shoes, and drug peddling. Because of their increasing numbers, the efforts of nongovernmental organizations, and media attention, street children are now commanding a great deal of attention in India. My discussion here is based on a review of studies carried out on this group (aged five to eighteen years), as well as information taken from newspaper and magazine reports.

There are an estimated eleven million street children in India, with their numbers ranging from fifty to one hundred thousand in the metropolitan cities (Delhi, Calcutta, Bombay, Madras) and fifteen to twenty-five thousand in smaller cities (Indore, Hyderabad, Kanpur, Pune) (Phillips, 1992). Reasons for child work are chronic poverty, migration, unemployment, overcrowded homes, parental abuse, drug abuse, alcoholism, parents abandoning children because of economic pressure, and children running away from stressful home situations (Fonseka and Malhotra, 1994; Ghosh, 1992; Reddy, 1992).

The existence of street children is essentially an urban phenomenon. Their families migrate from rural, drought-hit, or flood-affected areas in search of better employment prospects. Most of the children come from second- and third-generation migrant families and from the lower castes and socially disadvantaged groups. However, Bombay and Delhi also have child migrants from other countries, including Bangladesh, Tibet, and Pakistan (Panicker and Nangia, 1992). Street children often belong to large families (six to ten members) and families that report an average income of less than 1,000 rupees per month (about $24 at the current exchange rate) (Institute of Psychological and Educational Research, 1991). Studies reveal that almost half of Indian street children do not have a roof over their heads and lack access to basic amenities (Rane and Shroff, 1994). They reside with or without their families on street pavements, beneath flyovers, at railway stations, under bridges, at bus stops, in temples, and in market areas in the cities.

Most street children in India are not rootless or unattached, and a majority (90 percent) live with their parents or other family members (Arimpoor, 1992; Verma and Dhingra, 1993). The remaining children may have distant family contacts or have been abandoned and hence are living on their own. However, the ratio varies, and more children live on their own in cities like Delhi, Calcutta, Bombay, Madras, and Indore (D'Lima and Gosalia, 1992; Ghosh, 1992; Panicker and Nangia, 1992).

Children start working on the streets very young. Almost one-third of street children are six to eleven years old, and 40 percent are twelve to fifteen years old. There are more boys than girls on the streets. Girls start working earlier, and they stop earlier because of early marriage (Fonseka and Malhotra, 1994). Very few postpubertal girls are found on the streets, possibly because girls who have not married may have been lured into prostitution (Rane and Shroff, 1994).

Most street children are illiterate and unskilled, lacking the resources and motivation to go to school. Estimates indicate that about 63 percent of the children work eight to twelve hours a day (Rane and Shroff, 1994). The average daily income of about 70 percent of street children is around 10 rupees (24 cents), and approximately 30 percent of the children do not have any rest period (Institute of Psychological and Educational Research, 1991). Middlemen and policemen often exploit these children and subject them to physical abuse, confiscate their daily earnings, and make them do odd chores. The more fortunate of these children find jobs selling newspapers or lottery tickets or working as tea shop attendants and helpers in automobile repair shops (Mathur, 1993). When all else fails, they resort to begging, thieving, peddling drugs, pimping, and even scrounging from the garbage (Koushik and Bawikar, 1990; Varma and Jain, 1992). Harsh weather conditions during winter and monsoons force children to migrate to other cities. Many children go from Delhi to Bombay during winter, and children from Bombay come to Delhi during monsoons (Panicker and Nangia, 1992).

Street life often affects the health of these children. Street children often suffer from bacterial and parasitic infections such as cholera, typhoid, gastroenteritis, amoebic dysentery, tetanus, tuberculosis, ringworm, scabies, and rickets. Many of them are covered in cuts and bruises, sustained during street fights, accidents, or confrontation with authorities. Lacking adequate nourishment, many children suffer from malnutrition and show symptoms of stunted growth, anemia, and night blindness (Sekar and Pinto, 1992). Additional health hazards are related to prostitution and the use of alcohol and drugs. The worldwide increased involvement of young girls and boys in prostitution, in India as elsewhere, has been accompanied by an increase in the incidence of sexually transmitted diseases (Bouhdiba, 1981). Recent newspaper articles on the work of children in Asia have contained horrifying details about the increasing notoriety of the "child sex worker" industry: "Brothel owners are eagerly seeking child prostitutes as there is less risk of exposure and jail and in the fond hope that sex with young children means less risk for AIDS" (Rao, 1997). Street children are also easy victims for drug peddlers. Cases of drug abuse are reported from Delhi, Bangalore, Bombay, and Madras, where a small percentage of the children are addicts of brown sugar, heroin, and marijuana. Children are often rounded up by the police and, if found to be drug users, are exposed to severe corporal punishment (Institute of Psychological and Educational Research, 1991). In sum, life on the streets puts children's health and their very survival in danger.

## Activity Patterns of Daily Life

A major concern of mine has been to identify and understand the different experiential settings that make up the daily lives of working street children. What goes on in these settings? What risks do they present? How might they provide opportunities for the development of skills and competencies? Determining the amount of time street children spend in different activities and locations and with different persons provides a beginning index for the typical action patterns and social experiences of these children (Barker and Wright, 1955).

To study street children's daily experiences, my students and I engaged in three consecutive studies on time allocation over a period of two years (Verma and Bhan, 1996). These studies were carried out in Chandigarh, a mid-sized city in which most street children return to sleep with their families in empty lots each evening. The objectives of the studies were, first, to evolve a methodology to study time use of street children and, second, to develop a time use profile of street children for different periods (morning, midday, afternoon, evening, and night) by occupation and gender. The sample for the final study, from which our results were derived, consisted of one hundred children and adolescents, aged eight to eighteen years, who were working on the streets as beggars, vendors, and ragpickers or in other occupations. Time use data were gathered through three games and through "time diary" interviews, both involving recall of activities from the prior day.

The results show that street children are involved in a multitude of differing activities from dawn to dusk; that significant gender differences occur, with girls spending more time in housework and street work and less time in leisure; that children combine work and leisure when on the street; that friends and siblings emerge as the group of companions with whom street children most often interact; that parental supervision occurs only during the performance of household chores; that the child on the street spends one-third of the day at home and two-thirds in public places; that earning activities are associated with neutral emotions and sometimes feelings of sadness or irritability, along with a neutral level of motivation; and that leisure activities evoke positive average feelings and positive motivation. We can see the developmental opportunities and limits of these patterns by looking more closely at specific activities.

**Household Work.** These children's household activities include child care, cleaning, cooking, washing, fetching water, and collecting wood or fuel, among other things. Child care is generally combined with other activities, and often beggar children and ragpickers are seen caring for younger siblings at their workplace, such as market areas. Girls as young as six years are found independently taking care of infants. Girls spend almost four times more time than boys engaged in household chores (four to five hours per day). Most of these activities take place during early morning or late evening hours since most of the day is spent at the workplace. Boys do more outdoor household tasks and errands, whereas girls more often work in close proximity to their living area. Thus domestic work follows gender stereotypes, resulting in grooming for adult male and female roles. These early role responsibilities, however, are accompanied by an underdeveloped maturity for skill acquisition (girls as young as six or seven are seen cooking on fires, bathing an infant, and dressing wounds), which, along with the repetitive nature of household chores, limits the developmental opportunities of these activities.

**Income-Earning Activities.** Children drift out to the street between the ages of four and five, accompanying their older siblings. They engage in a wide variety of marginal economic activities that vary according to the weather, season, and other factors. Children in our study spent eight to ten hours per day on the streets combining work with play and rest. Working hours are flexible, and the peak hours of work vary by the activity. Ragpickers leave their homes as early as 5 A.M. in the summer and remain at garbage dump areas until late in the evening, often walking eight to twelve kilometers (five to seven miles) in a day. Beggars, vendors, shoe shiners, and car cleaners have their peak working hours during the evening and are a common sight in market areas until long after dark. Girls generally return home early, whereas boys work until late at night.

Children, especially boys, also spend time in activities not directly related to their street trade, which may or may not have monetary benefits. These activities include doing work for shopkeepers—running errands and guarding goods—for which rewards may be in kind or just an assurance of protection from police. With little adult supervision and limited alternatives available, children learn to fend for themselves. Collaborations with peers can lead to the formation of gangs. Membership in the gang is important, especially for beggar and ragpicking children, who have clear-cut working "boundaries." Any violation of the rules invites serious fights among groups, and social ostracism is used as a form of reprimand (Pande, 1992; Verma and Dhingra, 1993).

**Leisure Time Activities.** In the lives of street children there is no clear-cut demarcation of time for leisure and work: they are often combined and carried out with same-gender siblings and friends. Typical leisure activities were found to include talking and chatting, playing games, roaming around, watching television, dancing, singing, listening to transistor radios, playing video games in market areas, watching movies, and playing in parks or open areas. Children, especially boys, typically watched at least two or three movies per week and emulated the heroes as role models. Younger children often created their own toys by manipulating material used by adults to make dolls, balls, or replicas of objects found in their immediate environment, such as earthen utensils and tools. Their role-play activities include separating rags, fetching water, and cooking using tiny containers, thus imitating elder siblings and mothers. This role-play of adult tasks can be viewed as a normal education process and illustrates the way in which these children actively participate in their own socialization.

**Implications for Skill Development.** Street children are "the quintessential *karmayogis*, they live for the moment without thought for the future" (Thapa, 1995, p. 177). The thrill of street life and freedom of action and movement are typical images that emerged from the daily accounts of these street children. In their daily lives, skill learning is informal, play is unstructured, playmates are workmates, and time spent on the streets teaches children useful life skills. These skills include relatedness, negotiation skills, stress management, personal safety skills, leisure time management, and dealing with abuse and aggression—in an environment full of physical, moral, and emotional risks. Girls are more stressed than boys, with dual responsibilities at home and at work. Street gang affiliation provides a sense of identity to the child in which courage, independence, and rebelliousness are valued qualities.

Lack of parental protection and guidance for a large part of the day characterizes street children's daily activities, which has led me to look more closely at the nature of the interactions that street children do have with their families and what role they play in children's development of cognitive skills, moral judgment, and coping.

## Socialization for Survival: Role of the Family

Situational analysis of street children in India clearly reveals that economic pressures on the family and family crises force children to make the streets their abode for survival. In such families, values and aspirations are congruent with the demands and limitations imposed by the immediate environment. Parents' attitudes toward children's work, other roles, and socialization reflect the economic, social, and cultural framework within which these families function. Family life is shaped by the hazards of street life, which combine with multiple risk indicators, such as poverty, minority status, violence, lack of schooling, substance abuse, displacement, hopelessness, single parenthood, and abuse. Households experience repeated crises of health, unemployment, and criminality (Blanc, 1994). Alcoholism is common among fathers. Human relationships under such conditions frequently suffer, and children do not receive as much attention as they should. Due to lack of adequate supervision, many children lead a semi-independent life from an early age (Fonseka and Malhotra, 1994), increasing the prospects of being led astray into social evils. Such factors in the family setting are likely to have adverse effects on parent-child relations and affect the coping styles and personality development of the child.

**Parent-Child Relationship.** For most of the world's children, the parent-child relationship provides stability, financial security, health care, education, and training in morality and respect (Katz, 1971). Yet problems can arise when parents fail to perform these functions, especially when they move in and out of crisis situations that demand massive adjustments (Tower, 1993). Studies evaluating the quality of the parent-child relationship among street children in India have focused on children's and parents' perceptions of each other.

The findings present a mixed picture. The majority of street children report feeling loved and wanted by their parents. They share their problems with parents, are taken care of when ill, enjoy joint recreational activities, and obtain from parents advice on problems and praise for their good qualities (Phillips, 1992; Rao and Mallick, 1992; Reddy, 1992). However, children also report frequent disputes with their parents over low earnings, family problems, disobedience, keeping money aside, and watching movies (Verma and Dhingra, 1993).

The teaching style of these parents is based on observation, imitation, and demonstration, rather than verbal explanation and logical reasoning. The learning of socially prescribed roles and skills necessary for earning on the streets is reinforced (Verma and Kumar, 1996). The learning of self-care and work-related skills, however, is context-dependent. Street children learn skills that are functional for daily problem solving in the street context, but parental emphasis is more on learning specific task mastery skills, and this may not always facilitate transfer of learning. Kagitçibasi (1996) argues that this type of everyday procedural learning is limited, especially when social structural changes (urban-rural mobility, shifts in economic activities and job markets) require development of new types of cognitive skills and competencies.

In the culture of street families, feelings are expressed through behavior and action rather than by touch or words. Compared to middle-class parents, their parents use less verbal interaction, less praise, and more directives and negative physical control, which may disadvantage the cognitive development of the child. Very often nonrestrictive discipline stressing independence and autonomy is the norm; however, in areas of conflict, parents predominantly use physical assertion with children (Verma and Kumar, 1996; Vij, 1990).

In a comparative analysis of the conditions of street children in five countries (Brazil, Kenya, India, Italy, and the Philippines), Blanc (1994) concludes that most working street children come from poor, stressed, but still reasonably supportive households. Street children living with their families, when compared to those living on their own, appeared relatively less subject to severe problems with less incidence of malnutrition, substance abuse, and family violence. The presence of caring adults, overburdened and stressed as they may be, still provides a buffer during emotional crises.

**Morality and Development of Values.** A related family function is transmitting moral values to children. Research in the United States suggests that frequent use of power assertion by mothers is consistently associated with less advanced moral development and use of induction with more advanced moral development (Hoffman and Saltzstein, 1972). In a study of Indian beggar children, Vij (1990) found age-appropriate levels of moral judgment (according to Kohlberg's stages), despite their mothers' use of power assertion as a predominant disciplinary practice. Vij speculates that early independence, training in survival skills, and the shouldering of multiple responsibilities, such as child care, may promote moral development in these children. Peer interaction also provides experiences in reciprocal role taking, mutual respect, group solidarity, empathy, and a more internalized understanding of others' needs. These experiences may stimulate the developmental progression in beggar children from moral realism to moral reciprocity at a rate comparable to their middle-class counterparts. These children beg, it should be understood, not because they do not know the difference between ethically desirable and undesirable behavior but because they do not have many alternatives.

While moral judgment may be developed, other research suggests a less positive picture for moral behavior and values. Some studies report increasing incidence of antisocial behavior in street children with age (Panicker and Nangia, 1992; Phillips, 1992). Development of values may be affected in street children because they come from families where priority is placed on immediate gratification of needs and desires, where parental guidance is minimal or nonexistent (Verma and Bhan, 1996), and where some adults model undesirable behavior (Sekar and Pinto, 1992). Children may be unable to decide which models to emulate and quite naturally behave in a manner that will get them the most immediate gratification from the situation. These children, therefore, become too independent too fast with too few ethical guidelines about how to use their independence. Many end up using their independence to satisfy physical needs first and, like significant adults in their environments, start smoking, drinking, taking drugs, and indulging in sexual activities much earlier than other children (Dubey, 1985).

**Coping with Stress and Abuse.** Childhood and adolescence are critical times for the acquisition of coping and social skills. This process depends on having positive attachments, the opportunity and resources to learn the skills, and an absence of overwhelming stressful situations. The contrary also holds. Lack of skills and coping are readily transmitted to the next generation, particularly where families provide low-quality and inconsistent support to children, provide behavioral models of substance abuse, lack closeness and involvement in their children's activities, have low educational aspirations, exert weak control and discipline, and abuse their children emotionally, physically, or sexually. When these latter circumstances occur, one form of response is for children to take to the streets, where other street children provide a sense of belonging to a new and often more caring replacement "family" (Belsey, 1996).

Studies reveal that Indian street children experience a high incidence of stress and physical abuse in their families (Institute of Psychological and Educational Research, 1991), and for many children, this is the reason for abandoning families and making a transition to street living (Ghosh, 1992). Gil (1970) suggests that environmental stress is largely responsible for child abuse. Factors such as poor education, poverty, racism, unemployment, marital disputes, and occupational stress weaken parents' self-control and may result in abusive behavior. Failure to meet the child's physical as well as psychological needs can lead parents to aggressive expressions of frustration, anger, and hostility (Mathur and Mittal, 1996). The child's perception of absent family support further complicates the situation and can create feelings of alienation, leading to hostility and personality disorders (Gupta and Verma, 1996). In such stressful situations, children are often overly aggressive and may turn to drugs or alcohol, become delinquent, or demonstrate dependency with little underlying trust (Tower, 1993). This may hamper the child's abilities to form satisfying relationships within and outside the home, leading to impaired social skills, feelings of inferiority, submissiveness, low life aspirations, and low achievement motivation (Mathur and Sabharwal, 1996; Reddy, 1992).

Studies conducted in Chandigarh, however, suggest a different trend in the coping mechanism of street children. Using a multimethod approach (observation, drama, feedback), Gupta (1995) helped street children identify stressful situations in their daily lives in the domains of work, earnings, home, school, peers, and siblings. Results revealed that these children used emotion-focused, escape-avoidant coping strategies when confronted with immutable authority figures, such as policemen, middlemen at the workplace, and parents. They used problem-focused coping in situations related to loss of income due to illness, bad weather, holidays, and low sales, where they have some control of the situation. When confronted with problems with peers and siblings, once again problem-focused coping styles were used. The author argues that these children are learning to cope in situationally appropriate ways: they are able to see most stressful situations as challenges rather than threats.

In a related study of street children in Chandigarh, we studied the preference for social support in stressful situations (Gupta and Verma, 1996). Children were shown photographs of possible social contacts whose support they could seek when faced with stress and asked how they would respond. Results revealed that children preferred to be alone or seek support of peers in problems related to the workplace, and they preferred support from mothers when in need of money and to deal with sibling- or household-related problems. More boys preferred to deal with problems on their own, whereas more girls sought their mothers' support. Children preferred their grandparents and other relatives only in situations where parents had a dispute. On the whole, these children formulated responses to stressful situations that showed a great deal of competence, self-reliance, and adaptive skills.

**Implications for Skill Development.** These children are truly being socialized for survival. In impoverished families with frequent conflict, the childhood period is short, and children are initiated early into the world of work and family responsibilities. Children develop skills related to household work, earning, and dealing with daily stresses, although lack of training in transferable cognitive skills limits future job opportunities and upward mobility. With learning opportunities severely limited and the possibility of entering school closed, the street child is being surely prepared for the illiterate, unskilled labor market (Naidu, 1985). Although children do develop the capacity for moral reasoning, the models and demands of the street do not consistently promote moral behavior, which exposes them to higher risk.

Nevertheless, children perceive their families as supportive in periods of crisis, and most youth demonstrate the development of coping skills suited to surviving within their difficult daily environment. Left with few options but to behave as "little adults on the streets," they exhibit remarkable relationship skills in dealing with adults in public. They demonstrate wit and presence of mind in conflict situations. In sum, these children develop survival strategies beyond their level of developmental maturity, yet there are developmental costs and certainly a cost to their well-being.

## Conclusions

What do the life experiences of street children in India as captured in this chapter tell us? Lost childhood! Blossoms in the dust! Premature adulthood! Children at risk! Several developmental issues emerge:

- Health, physical development, and mortality are unquestionably the most serious issues associated with child street work activity.
- The manual work children do is repetitive, monotonous, and hazardous, offering little opportunity for learning skills that transfer to more remunerative, safer, or more rewarding occupations. Street work often precludes school attendance and thus interferes with development of the cognitive skills necessary for entry into the wider society.
- Family cohesiveness, despite stresses, alienation, and marginalization, provides an important safety network for many children. Although some parents are unable to cope with the demands of parenting, many families and children show extraordinary resilience in the face of poverty and harsh physical and economic conditions.
- In the case of children who leave home, a breakdown in the functional role of the family means inadequate socialization, a loss of affectional ties, dysfunctional or damaging relationships, and antisocial behavior, thus affecting the psychosocial competency of the child.
- Street life outside the supervision of parental authority or an educational institution places the child at greater risk of associating with deviant peers and lowers the threshold for engaging in health-risking and antisocial behaviors, such as drug and alcohol use, sexual activity, robbery, and violence. Children embark on a negative developmental trajectory that will perpetuate the harm.

**Proposals for Research.** Several crucial but underresearched analytical issues can be identified:

- The life conditions of street children raise complex methodological obstacles that limit the value of traditional research approaches. We need to adopt multimethod, multifaceted interdisciplinary approaches relying on qualitative as well as quantitative research strategies to ensure that the reality of the street children's situation does not elude us.
- We need a deeper understanding of the street child's family dynamics, traditions, and conditions for socialization. Knowledge is needed on continuity and change in family patterns, proximal and distal relations of the child to the family, and the emotional and cognitive strategies that families adopt for orientation and survival.
- We need to focus questions on childhood abuse and trauma, stress experiences, and alternate developmental pathways adopted by street children.
- Special focus needs to be given to the coping strategies of the child of the street who has severed all ties with the family or has been orphaned.
- Finally, we need more cross-cultural studies and sharing of databases on street children around the world to facilitate networking among professionals. Such networking will permit the sharing of success stories and innovative strategies to deal with the growing phenomenon of children in difficult circumstances.

**Future Action.** The antithesis of "street" is "home" (Black, 1991). The institutional approach to helping street children is by and large a repressive, correctional one and has proved to be ineffective in terms of long-term rehabilitation, especially where there is lack of follow-up services (Blanc, 1994). Hostile and punitive attitudes toward street children and their families must be replaced by more need-based, child-centered initiatives. Delivery systems must reach out to families to strengthen the capacity of both the family and the community to provide a nurturing environment for children and a head start for life. Innovative strategies can tackle the problem of poverty with empowerment and income generation options for families, whereas others may try to restore the child's right to health, education, and development. Multiple entry points in schools, open education, and access to functional literacy programs can go a long way in ameliorating the conditions of children in distress. One such example is that of the Urban Basic Services for the Poor initiated by UNICEF for addressing the problem of India's slum children within a community-focused framework.

To end with the words of Black (1991, p. 22): "The key to understand the child's predicament is to recognize the price paid, in physical well-being, in skills and intellectual development, in socially empathic behavior, in moral values, by being cut off at too early an age from a structured life style, loving nurture and support. It is the degree of that deprivation, and the distance the child has drifted from integration in the family setting, which above all determines whether street life—even when it teaches useful survival skills—becomes for that child the social and personal disaster the phrase tends to conjure."

# References

Arimpoor, J. *Street Children of Madras: A Situational Analysis.* Noida, India: Child Labour Cell, National Labour, 1992.

Barker, R. G., and Wright, H. F. *Midwest and Its Children.* New York: HarperCollins, 1955.

Belsey, M. A. "The Child and the Family: New Challenges to Accelerating Change." *International Child Health*, 1996, 7(3), 19.

Black, M. *Children of the Runaway Cities.* Paris: UNICEF, 1991.

Blanc, C. S. "Some Comparative Trends: Street, Work, Hopelessness, Schooling and Survival Strategies." In C. S. Blanc (ed.), *Urban Children in Distress.* London: Gordon & Breach, 1994.

Bouhdiba, A. W. *Exploitation of Child Labour.* New York: United Nations Commission on Human Rights, 1981.

Burra, N. *Born to Work: Child Labour in India.* Delhi, India: Oxford University Press, 1997.

D'Lima, H., and Gosalia, R. *Street Children of Bombay: A Situational Analysis.* Noida, India: Child Labour Cell, National Labour, 1992.

Dube, L. "The Economic Roles of Children in India: Methodological Issues." In G. Rodgers and G. Standing (eds.), *Child Work, Poverty and Underdevelopment.* Geneva: International Labor Office, 1981.

Dubey, E. V. "Personality Development of Working Children." In U. S. Naidu and K. R. Kapadia (eds.), *Child Labour and Health.* Bombay, India: Tata Institute of Social Sciences, 1985.

Fonseka, L., and Malhotra, D. D. "India: Urban Poverty, Children and Participation." In C. S. Blanc (ed.), *Urban Children in Distress.* London: Gordon & Breach, 1994.

Ghosh, A. *Street Children of Calcutta.* Noida, India: Child Labour Cell, National Labour, 1992.

Gil, D. *Violence Against Children.* Cambridge, Mass.: Harvard University Press, 1970.

Gupta, A. "Coping Responses and Preference for Social Support in Daily Life Stressful Situations by Children and Adolescents on the Street." Master's dissertation, Panjab University, Chandigarh, India, 1995.

Gupta, A., and Verma, S. "Preference for Social Support by Indian Street Children and Adolescents in Stressful Life Situations." Presentation at the Fourteenth Biennial Meeting of the International Society for the Study of Behavioral Development, Quebec, Canada, Aug. 12–16, 1996.

Hoffman, M. L., and Saltzstein, H. D. "Parent Discipline and Child's Moral Development." In R. C. Johnson, P. R. Dockecki, and O. M. Mowrer (eds.), *Conscience, Concept, and Social Reality.* New York: Holt, Rinehart and Winston, 1972.

Institute of Psychological and Educational Research. *A Composite Report of Situational Analysis of Urban Street Children in India.* Calcutta, India: Institute of Psychological and Educational Research, 1991.

Kagitçibasi, C. *Family and Human Development Across Cultures.* Mahwah, N.J.: Erlbaum, 1996.

Katz, S. N. *When Parents Fail.* Boston: Beacon Press, 1971.

Koushik, S. S., and Bawikar, R. *Street Children of Pune City: A Status Report, 1990.* Pune, India: Karve Institute of Social Service, 1990.

Mathur, M. "Mapping Socioeconomic Realities of Street Children in Jaipur, India." In K. Ekberg and P. E. Mjaavatn (eds.), *Children at Risk: Selected Papers.* Trondheim, Norway: University of Trondheim, 1993.

Mathur, M., and Mittal, D. "Deprivation, Aggression and Reactions to Frustrations in Street Children of Jaipur City, India." Presentation at the Fourteenth Biennial Meeting of the International Society for the Study of Behavioral Development, Quebec, Canada, Aug. 12–16, 1996.

Mathur, M., and Sabharwal, A. "Level of Aspirations and Achievement Motivation in Street Children." In S. Grover (ed.), *Researches in Human Development.* Jaipur, India: Rupa Books, 1996.

Mendelievich, E. "Introductory Analysis." In E. Mendelievich (ed.), *Children at Work*. Geneva: International Labor Office, 1980.

Naidu, U. S. "Health Problems of Working Children: Some Issues in Planning Long Term Care." In U. S. Naidu and K. R. Kapadia (eds.), *Child Labour and Health: Problems and Prospects*. Bombay, India: Tata Institute of Social Sciences, 1985.

Nair, M., and Taraporevala, S. *Salaam Bombay*. New Delhi, India: Penguin Books, 1989.

Pande, R. *Street Children of Kanpur*. Noida, India: Child Labour Cell, National Labour, 1992.

Panicker, R., and Nangia, P. *Working and Street Children of Delhi*. Noida, India: Child Labour Cell, National Labour, 1992.

Phillips, W.S.K. *Street Children of Indore*. Noida, India: Child Labour Cell, National Labour, 1992.

Rane, A. J., and Shroff, N. "Street Children in India: Emerging Need for Social Work Intervention." In A. J. Rane (ed.), *Street Children*. Bombay, India: Tata Institute of Social Sciences, 1994.

Rao, B.V.R., and Mallick, B. *Street Children of Hyderabad*. Noida, India: Child Labour Cell, National Labour, 1992.

Rao, R. "Indian Children in Vice Den." *Chandigarh Tribune,* Jan. 11, 1997.

Reddy, N. *Street Children of Bangalore*. Noida, India: Child Labour Cell, National Labour, 1992.

Sekar, H. R., and Pinto, G. J. *Situation of Working Children in Tamil Nadu*. Noida, India: Child Labour Cell, National Labour, 1992.

Sinha, D. "Towards an Ecological Framework of Deprivation." In D. Sinha, R. C. Tripathi, and G. Mistra (eds), *Deprivation: Its Social Roots and Psychological Consequences*. New Delhi, India: Concept, 1982.

Thapa, V. J. "Skilled Survivors." *India Today,* Mar. 31, 1995.

Tower, C. S. *Understanding Child Abuse and Neglect*. Needham Heights, Mass.: Allyn & Bacon, 1993.

Varma, A. P., and Jain, M. *Situation of Working Children in Uttar Pradesh*. Noida, India: Child Labour Cell, National Labour, 1992.

Verma, S., and Bhan, T. P. *Daily Life Activities in the Physical and Social Milieu of Indian Street Children*. Paper presented at the Fourteenth Biennial Meeting of the International Society for the Study of Behavioral Development, Quebec, Canada, Aug. 12–16, 1996.

Verma, S., and Dhingra, G. "Who Do They Belong To? A Profile of Street Children in Chandigarh." *People's Action,* 1993, 8(1), 22–25.

Verma, S., and Kumar, S. "Quality of Family Life Experiences and Work Related Problems of Street Children." Presentation at the Sixth Biennial Meeting of the Society for Research on Adolescence, Boston, Mar. 7–10, 1996.

Vij, R. *Moral Judgement and Perceived Maternal Disciplinary Practices in Beggar Children*. Master's dissertation, Department of Child Development, Panjab University, Chandigarh, India, 1990.

Weiner, M. *The Child and the State in India*. Delhi, India: Oxford University Press, 1991.

SUMAN VERMA *teaches at the Department of Child Development, Government Home Science College, Panjab University, Chandigarh, India.*

*Brazilian kids living on the streets of large urban centers face an immediate social reality that limits their identities to that of "little criminals." This reality rarely offers them chances to experiment with more socially acceptable selves and, most important, to believe they can become fuller human beings.*

# Daily Reality on the Streets of Campinas, Brazil

*Marcelo Diversi, Ney Moraes filho, Margareth Morelli*

"Do you know that this is bad for your health?" I heard the juvenile officer say to Drigo with concern.

"Do you know that crack drives your hunger and fear away?" Drigo shot back at the officer. "And it's soooo fun!" he said, chuckling.

"This stuff will kill you soon," the officer retorted, shaking his head.

"Unless a bullet does it first," Drigo said casually, looking at his own reflection on a window pane and fixing his black wavy hair.

*Notes from June 9, 1996, Campinas*

Most people, including many who work directly with them, seem unable to understand how pressing needs shape Brazilian street kids' immediate reality and affect their choices and behavior. For instance, most people see crack consumption mainly as a threat to health or a result of some psychological predicament, whereas kids living on the streets see crack primarily as a feasible way of fighting hunger, fear, and a bleak existence. One serious consequence of this mismatch in perceptions of reality is that intervention programs have very often failed to address the needs of kids living on the streets, or at least to provide attractive alternatives to their street lives. Institutions and shelters find their programs emptied and discontinued, while the streets of downtown are crowded with kids making their home there. As a result, kids living on the streets continue to have little or no access to a healthier development. The main goal of this chapter is to shed light on the immediate reality experienced by kids living on the streets of downtown Campinas, Brazil, offering a glimpse at the actual world so many boys and girls face on a daily basis.

This knowledge is of crucial importance if we are to understand the sociopsychological context in which street kids develop. Quoting Steinberg, "In order to understand how adolescents develop in contemporary society, [one] needs first to understand the world in which adolescents live and how that world affects their behavior and social relationships" (1996, p. xv).

To do so, we first present a brief overview of historical and political forces shaping the social reality that in turn shapes the lives of these kids. Next, we present ethnographic information on the more immediate world encountered by street kids in the city of Campinas. We then present an ethnographic account that attempts to make their world more meaningful to the reader. We end with a brief remark on some potential developmental effects that growing up in that world may have on kids' cognition and identity.

## Historical Background

Brazil's recent history was heavily marked by twenty-one years of military rule, starting with a coup in 1964 and ending in 1985 when the congress elected a nonmilitary president. Claiming a need to fight "internal enemies," and based on a militarist notion that the government must decide what is best for the population, the military government formulated a constitution in 1967 giving the executive sector power over the legislative and judiciary sectors. This imbalance enabled the military regime to create repressive measures and institutions with legal authority to imprison and use violence against citizens perceived as subversive.

As censorship and repression continued, the more privileged segments of society organized and were able to regain political influence and personal liberties for themselves. But in the meantime, the repressive apparatus had already become pervasive in the fabric of social life and had shifted its targets from the sons and daughters of the middle-class to those of the less economically privileged. Although in the late 1970s, police raids at the homes of dissident politicians and intellectuals decreased and mechanisms of repression were slowly deactivated because of internal and external pressures from human rights movements, the poorest sectors of the population continued to suffer the repressive measures implemented by the military regime.

One of the most striking examples of the measures implemented by the military, which still affects the poor, is the *Código de Menores* (Minors' Code), a legal code aimed at punishing deviant actions committed by individuals under eighteen years old. The Minors' Code, created in 1968 at the pinnacle of military repression, gave broad powers to the authorities to discipline and punish children and adolescents in closed reformatories, while containing no provisions for educational programs to empower and reintegrate the youngsters into society. Under the Minors' Code, intimidation and physical and emotional violence became the norm for handling minors among police and reformatory personnel (da Silva, 1996). Minors convicted of all types of infractions were institutionalized under the same conditions in the same places; kids caught for merely roaming the streets were locked up with those convicted of violent crimes—and treated equally badly.

The Minors' Code made the kids of the urban poor especially vulnerable. In the process of migrating from rural to urban areas, many poor families had lost social networks essential for the care and monitoring of children. Unemployment and extremely low-paying jobs made it necessary for many kids to go to the streets in search of extra income. Subhuman living conditions and a precarious school system forced many kids to spend many hours a day on the streets without adult supervision. Children and adolescents wearing torn clothes, often shoeless and dirty, walking aimlessly around business and richer areas, were likely candidates for reformatories just for fitting the delinquent profile described by the Minors' Code (da Silva, 1996).

The Minors' Code was officially replaced in 1990 by a far more humanistic and educationally oriented set of laws, the *Estatuto da Criança e do Adolescente* (Statute for Children and Adolescents), or *ECA*. But the daily existence of kids living on the streets is still marked by the repressive residues of the Minors' Code. For instance, these kids are often turned away or expelled from shelters without explanation, even though the ECA states that such actions are illegal and subject to criminal punishment. Many juvenile courts and their officers, trained under the Minors' Code, seem unwilling to operate based on the new laws. Thus most street kids do not benefit from the new protection established by the ECA.

In addition to having a history of repression of the poor, the Brazilian federal government never developed a welfare system. Social welfare in Brazil has always relied on charity, mostly of religious groups. Nongovernmental organizations (NGOs) have formulated and developed their programs based on their own idiosyncratic views of childhood and adolescence (heavily influenced by the authoritarianism of the Minors' Code). As a result, programs have been shaped much more by religious notions of salvation through work and prayer than by scientific knowledge on child and adolescent development.

The religious NGOs, which constitute the overwhelming majority of institutions working with street kids in Brazil, are formed mainly by volunteers from sponsoring churches. These volunteers draw for the most part on their own parenting experiences and religious faith to deal with kids who have had very different life experiences. Volunteers tend to lack understanding of the kids' struggles for independence and survival in the hostile environment they face on the streets and often perceive drug use, prostitution, petty crimes, and street language as expressions of moral weakness and lack of divine enlightenment. The result is often a mismatch of social realities, leading to the abandonment of their programs by the kids they desire to serve.

As a result of this situation, most large urban centers have seen an increase in the number of kids on the streets. According to various estimates, the number of street kids in Brazil ranges from 7 to 30 million (Barker and Knaul,

1991; Lusk, 1992; Sanders, 1987; UNICEF, 1989). In this chapter we will focus on kids living on the streets of downtown Campinas. Even though we do not attempt generalization, we believe that the reality encountered by street kids in Campinas shares many aspects with life on the street in other large Brazilian cities.

## The Situation in Campinas

Campinas, with approximately one million inhabitants and a large industrial economy, is the second largest city in the state of São Paulo, 50 miles west of the city of São Paulo. It is the home of two prestigious universities and has one of the highest rates of income per capita in the nation. It has an expanding service sector, which has contributed to the rapid growth of its population in the past decade.

Despite these positive socioeconomic indexes, the number of families in poverty has been increasing rapidly. A recent study by the Brazilian Institute of Geography and Statistics showed that the number of *favelas* (slum neighborhoods) has increased by 25 percent in the city since 1990. It also found that 10 percent of Campinas's families are headed by a person earning minimum wage (the equivalent of $100 per month) and that 25 percent of families have net monthly incomes below $200. To illustrate what these numbers actually mean: according to the federal government's official data, a family of four needs at least $110 per month solely to buy food to meet *minimum* nutritional standards.

Although the literature suggests that the phenomenon of street kids cannot be entirely explained by poverty (see Aptekar, 1994), the strain imposed on poor kids' families and communities by the lack of economic resources is a determining force in their daily experiences. Most dwellings for these families are shacks without running water and sewage lines, and many have no electricity. Law enforcement is scarce and the crime rate is high. Medical and dental care are virtually nonexistent. Kids have to attend decaying schools, some of which have four or five different groups of students rotating every day in a desperate effort to serve the largest number of kids with the limited resources available. Local communities do not have child care centers or recreational facilities to occupy the kids while parents are at work. Thus these kids are constrained by poverty in a large city such as Campinas—unless, of course, they start going to downtown.

**Coming to the Streets.** Downtown Campinas is inhabited mostly by middle- and upper-class families and concentrates a variety of businesses: offices, restaurants, bars, entertainment establishments, malls, supermarkets, stores, and street markets. It is a place crowded with shoppers, workers, people in transition, and economically privileged residents. Auto traffic is intense, and the intersections of large and busy avenues make a rare and unique setting for interaction between the begging and working poor and the wealthier population—a place where kids can make money by begging or selling overpriced candies and pens. It is also a place where food and a pair of shoes are often more easily obtained, by begging or stealing, than at home and where diversion seems practically endless. Eventually, for many kids, it may also become a place where money can be made through small thefts and a place to sleep can be found on benches, behind bushes, under trees, and beneath parked cars.

Kids come to the streets from several different situations, and their relationships with the streets vary greatly (see Raffaelli, 1997, for a review). Many kids are sent to the streets of downtown by their families to find food, money, or clothes (after school or all day if they do not attend school). Others go to the streets on their own but have silent support from their families, who are in need of the extra income provided by their youngsters. Some kids return home every evening, bringing along their daily gleanings. Some return home less often, if at all, and use their daily acquisitions for their own survival. Many kids living on the streets of downtown Campinas occasionally return to their parents' or relatives' homes for extended periods of time. The transition from home to street is often gradual: kids start going downtown for a few hours a day, then begin spending more time as they befriend kids already living on the streets. Our research suggests that kids who experience frequent violence at home tend to start spending the night on the streets sooner and more often than their counterparts from less violent homes.

The reasons for departure from home and communities and arrival in the streets are dependent on many variables, most of which are not currently known. The most attainable fact about this situation is that the number of kids coming of age in the streets of downtown Campinas is alarming by any available measure. In recent counts, estimates ranged from one hundred (from one conservative party in 1996) to five hundred (from the Workers' Party in 1994) to eight hundred (local NGOs in 1994). The individuals we will refer to in the rest of this chapter are among the fifty or so kids considered "hard core" by the local authorities. Most of these boys and girls, aged eleven to nineteen, have been on the streets for years, are addicted to crack, and have some history of legal infractions.

**Aggravating Problems.** In addition to lack of access to adequate services, the street kids' situation has been further jeopardized by the current epidemic of crack in Campinas, which started in the second half of 1994. Until that point, the main drugs consumed by street kids in Campinas were inhalants such as shoemaker's glue and nail polish. These drugs are potentially devastating in the long run (they can cause lung and brain damage) but do not have the immediate effects on kids' lives that crack has.

Kids find crack more appealing than inhalants for several reasons. First, according to kids we work with, it gets them higher and for a longer time. In addition, it is relatively cheap ($5 worth of crack is enough to get two kids high for a few hours) and easy to find. It also inhibits hunger, and many kids say they want the numbness crack gives them. "It's easier to get through the day when my head is full of crack," says Lucio, a fifteen-year-old boy who has been on the streets of downtown for several years. "I get less scared, you know; I can sleep well. And I don't give a damn about anything. I see a watch I want and I just snatch it and split."

On top of health problems such as extreme weight loss, tooth damage, and memory loss, the use of crack creates a physical dependency that forces kids to concentrate much of their energy on trying to obtain the drug (see Hatsukami and Fischman, 1996). We have observed sociological effects snowballing: kids started to steal more, many got involved in drug traffic in order to pay debts to dealers, and in turn the population and the police force have reacted more violently.

Instead of developing strategies to control the traffic of crack and to offer socioeducational alternatives for kids already living on the streets of downtown, the local government has spent money on the construction of juvenile prisons, on police enforcement, and on new technologies for identifying and punishing offenders. To be sure, the ECA has brought improvements that create at least a superficial awareness that street kids must be helped and not beaten. However, the apparatus and discourse of the Minors' Code are still predominant and expressed in Campinas through silently supported police brutality, popular labels such as "little criminals" and "future thieves," and the demonizing images of street kids widely circulated in the local media.

## Life as a Street Kid

Following methodological currents in interpretive ethnography (Denzin, 1997; Denzin and Lincoln, 1994; Jessor, Colby, and Shweder, 1996; Richardson, 1990, 1994), we now present an ethnographic account that seeks to present street kids' emic realities at an experiential level. We write this account as a story, with dialogues, unfolding action, and flashbacks, in an attempt to bring the reader as much as possible into their lived experiences. This account is a reconstruction of our encounters with kids in Campinas and our best effort to give voice to some of the street kids we have worked with.[1]

I saw Dalva crossing the street as I got off the bus. Dalva was carrying a brown bag in one hand and a can of Coke in the other. She was walking toward Rosario Plaza, and I rushed through the crowd to catch up with her. "Hey, Dalva, wait up!"

"Tio! You're in luck—I just got some food. Are you hungry?" she said between gulps of Coke.

Kids address anyone visibly older than they are as *Tio,* which means "Uncle" (or *Tia,* "Aunt"), and I was already getting used to it.

"No, thanks, Dalva, I just ate lunch." We walked together until she found shade under the trees on the quiet side of the plaza. She sat down and took a plate of commercial food out of the brown bag. "It looks good. Where did you get it?" I asked, looking at the small mountain of rice and beans on her plate.

"You know that new self-service restaurant they just opened next to that big bookstore?" she pointed, and I nodded yes. "Well, I was sitting by the door asking the people coming in and out of the restaurant for money. Then the manager came and said he would give me a plate of food if I went away, so I did." Dalva paused to stuff her mouth with food again. "But I guess I'm going back there again soon!" We looked at each other and laughed.

"You know, many restaurants now have security guards to keep us away," Dalva said, still eating. "Some security guys are nice and let us stay near the door for a while, but some are real mean. Did you hear what happened to Tate?"

I shook my head no, feeling from the tone of her voice that something bad had happened to him, imagining what it could be while she finished chewing. Tate was such a good-natured boy, always smiling and ready to tell some story about his "other life," as he used to refer to his life before coming to the streets of Campinas from a small town in a neighboring state. I never understood whether he left home because of an abusive stepfather or because he got a girl pregnant or because of other stories he only half told me. But I learned a great deal about farm animals, birds, and plants from his detailed and rich narratives. His travel adventures were told with gaiety and wit, and he had a special talent for making himself look like a fool without losing his dignity. People in downtown seemed to be especially fond of him, perhaps because of that. He was so peaceful that I had a hard time imagining that someone had harmed him.

"He got beat up real bad by that security guard working in front of the computer school, you know, near the restaurant where he is always watching customers' cars. He didn't do anything. This lady had just parked her car in front of the restaurant and he went up to her, asking if he could watch the car for her. You know, that's how he makes money. He doesn't steal or anything. But she must have thought he was gonna rob her and started screaming. You know how these rich people are—they see a dirty kid coming to talk to them and they're already thinking we're gonna rob 'em. So the security guy started pushing and punching Tate before he could say anything. Celi and I were the only kids around, and we were too afraid of getting beat up too. People started coming out of the shops to see what was going on. Some men started laughing at Tate. Nobody did anything to stop the beating. Poor Tate—he was all bloody and crying by the time the guy let go of him, and nobody did nothing. Then this man who was talking to the lady started coming toward us shouting that we should be in jail, that we should be . . . hmmm . . . how do you say . . . terminated?"

"Exterminated?"

"Yes, like those kids who were shot dead while sleeping by that church in Rio de Janeiro."

"What happened to Tate, then? Did he go to the hospital? You said he was bleeding. . . ."

"No, he said they would treat him bad at the hospital too because he was all dirty and smelly. Celi and I walked around to find a street educator to take him to the hospital but didn't find anyone. When we came back, Tate had disappeared. I haven't seen him since then. Nobody knows where he's hiding. Do you know that security guy?"

I shook my head no.

Dalva started eating again. I felt that she wanted me to go talk to him. But I didn't know what to do. We were in silence for a while. Then she wrapped the food left on the plate, some rice and beans and a chicken leg, with a napkin and put it inside the brown bag.

"I'm gonna take this food to Kleo and Grace. They are sleeping behind the post office and will wake up hungry," she said, getting up.

The post office is a large old building in one of the busiest areas of downtown. The wide sidewalks surrounding it are crowded with food and cheap merchandise stands, and right in front of its main entrance there is a bus stop connecting downtown with the working-class neighborhoods. It's a noisy place in the middle of the afternoon. "How can they get any sleep there?" I thought out loud.

"We didn't get much sleep last night," Dalva said, helping me to my feet.

The post office was only a few blocks from where we were, and as we walked, Dalva began telling me how they had been on the lookout for a woman dealer who was after them. "She said she's gonna kill us if we don't pay our crack debts, and we don't have any money. It's in the night that things happen, you know. So last night we kept on going from place to place, trying to stay awake."

Dalva told me they lay down at the doorstep of a pediatric clinic, but after a few minutes a police car stopped by and some cops came out and rousted them, saying they couldn't stay there. I had seen this clinic before. It had caught my attention one afternoon when I was looking for some of the kids. I remembered thinking that it was in an odd place, squeezed between a small clothing shop and a crumbling hotel where young women and men took their clients. I had stopped in front of it and read the sign with big yellow letters: WHERE WE CARE FOR THE CHILDREN OF CAMPINAS.

Dalva said they then walked to the church, lay down again, and the same cops came and kicked them out of there. The sun was already rising when they fell asleep in front of a vegetarian restaurant on a tiny street a little hidden from the busy streets of downtown. But at 10 A.M. the manager came to open it and woke them up.

"We then went to the post office and lay down by the back entrance, you know, where nobody goes. But the sun was cooking us and we couldn't fall asleep. Kleo and Grace rolled under a parked car and fell asleep in no time. I was too scared to fall asleep under the car—imagine if they didn't see us and just drove away! So I left and started looking for something to eat."

I shook my head, imagining.

We got to the post office, walking past food stands, lines of people waiting for buses, and men trying to sell lottery tickets. Going around the building to the back entrance, we saw Kleo and Grace under an old blue van. The blue van's chassis was really close to the ground, and I had to bend down to see the girls. I hadn't known many people who looked under the car before driving, so I understood exactly why Dalva was too afraid to join her friends. She put the brown bag next to Kleo, under the van, without waking them up, and sat down, leaning against the post office wall. I sat next to her, and we watched the van till the kids woke up.

The church bell had just struck 2 P.M. when Kleo and then Grace came out from under their urban tent carrying the brown bag with them. They sat down in front of us and, stretching and yawning, unwrapped the food.

"My hair is a mess, Tio," Grace said, pulling her black curly hair back with both hands. "Give me your cap, Tio, I don't want you to see me like this."

I took the cap off my head and gave it to her, saying that she looked fine. "Don't bullshit me, Tio. I know I look horrible. I'm all dirty and smelly and haven't washed my hair in days." She put my cap on and grabbed the cold chicken leg from the plate.

"They don't let us shower at Casa Aberta anymore, Tio," said Kleo with her mouth full of rice and beans.

"Yeah, but sometimes Tio Marcio lets us use the shower to clean up and wash our clothes," Dalva said.

"But only when the other staff members aren't there—those sonsabitches don't want us there anymore," Grace almost shouted between bites, just as a middle-aged couple walked out of the post office through the back entrance. They first looked at the three girls, their faces sulking, and said something I could not make out. But as they kept on walking away, the woman looked at me and asked, "What are *you* doing among these *moleques de rua*?" *Moleques de rua* ("street urchins") is a pejorative term, so I knew she wasn't really asking a question. I just watched as the couple disappeared into the crowd, hoping they couldn't hear Dalva and Grace showing off their repertoire of pejorative names for women.

"Can you take us to Casa Aberta, Tio? Maybe they will let us take a shower and wash our clothes if you talk to them," Kleo said after a while.

❧ ☙

I knew it'd be difficult to convince the people at Casa Aberta to let the girls use their facilities. I had taken Lara there the week before and heard the whole spiel about Casa Aberta's new policies. Casa Aberta, which literally means "open house," used to be a place where street kids could always go for a meal, a shower, and sometimes a session of occupational therapy. But feeling that Casa Aberta was serving as a crutch for kids who didn't want to commit to recovery, I was told by an administrator, they decided to change it into a halfway house for adult recovering addicts.

"Kids came here just for the food and shower, not wanting to stick to the hardships of recovery and salvation. We realized we were not helping them get off the streets but were instead keeping them dependent and unmotivated by being so lenient. We have now adopted the philosophy of tough love, so the kids have to prove they are really willing to stick to the program before they can go to the shelter," the same administrator told me. Then looking at Lara, who was standing next to me, "These kids need to know that everything has a price in life." Lara didn't smile back.

"And how can they prove their willingness if they are no longer allowed to come in here?" I wanted to ask.

"Lara has a doctor's appointment today and wants to clean up before going," I said.

Lara had told another street educator, a woman, that she thought she might be pregnant or have some venereal disease.

"So we were wondering if you could let her use your shower, just today, as a favor . . ." I was interrupted by Lara: "I don't have any other place to go, Tia! And I can't go to the doctor like this," she said pointing to her dirty bare feet.

The administrator, an older woman with short gray hair and a large wooden cross resting on her breasts, looked at Lara, touched her chin softly, and said that she was sorry but couldn't make an exception, that it wouldn't be fair to the other kids who were coming by for the same reason.

"I won't tell anybody, I promise!" Lara said.

"Sorry, honey, but I can't do that. . . ."

Lara's eyes watered. She turned around and started to walk away. I asked her not to leave, saying that we would find another place.

"Where? In your house?" she flung at me, crying. "All I want is to take a damn shower!" she shouted at the woman with a cross standing next to me and then bolted out of our sight. Lara was gone.

As the administrator talked about the problem of street children and the lack of love in their families, I tuned out and began wondering how I was going to tell the doctor that Lara wasn't going to make the appointment because we couldn't find a place for her to bathe.

Lara had just turned seventeen and had lived in foster homes since she was three years old, when her mother was sent to jail. She had just come to the streets again, after a quarrel with the young woman coordinating the Baptist female shelter where she was living. After a night on the streets of downtown, Lara tried to go back to the Baptist shelter and apologize for having left in anger. But the Baptist shelter was also following the tough love philosophy, and Lara was told she'd have to wait a week before being allowed to return. Her punishment was to spend a week on the streets so that she'd learn to appreciate what she had at the shelter.

"And they said I can't hang out with Dalva or Katia or Celi, or any other kids they think are bad, if I want to go back at all!" Lara said to me on the first night I saw her on the streets, with Dalva and Celi in front of a pizza place. "But I'm too afraid of being by myself here. I'm not used to making money on the streets, you know. I don't know how to steal and am too embarrassed to beg. I'm afraid someone I know will see me sleeping out here or dressed in rags." Here Lara was interrupted by Dalva.

"But somehow you always have new and clean clothes, nice shoes. . . . I wonder how you get the money for these things," Dalva said, affecting an innocent air.

Lara gave a mean look to Dalva, who then made a gesture of ironic apology. "It's not fair what they did, Tio. I apologized, on my knees, and they didn't believe me. I know I was wrong when I called her names and left the shelter. . . . I was angry. All I wanted to do was watch the soap opera, you know, that one that everybody's talking about. It was my birthday, so I thought I deserved to watch what I wanted and not that boring religious channel. . . . I know I have a bad temper, but I apologized. . . ." Lara started to cry softly.

"It's true, Tio, she doesn't know how to live on the streets," Dalva told me. "She can't even ask people for food, she gets too embarrassed, so I have to take care of her, right, Lara?"

"Yeah, Dalva got me some food tonight. I was starving."

"She started to cry, Tio," Dalva said, smiling a little.

"My stomach was hurting!" Lara replied.

"I know, I'm just teasing you, Lara. It's not right what they did to Lara, Tio!" Dalva told me, her face turning somber. "It's dangerous to be here alone, especially after dark, and I can't take her with me when I go buy crack, you see, the dealers don't like when people that don't smoke come with us—they think you are spying for the police, and that's bad business. So I have to leave her alone sometimes, or she'll have to come along and pretend she smokes too."

"I'm afraid to do that, Dalva."

"I know. . . . It's unfair what they did, you know? They say they want to help us, but they don't even know how! I wanted to see one of them rich goody-goody kids staying in that shelter—see how long they would last there!—and I bet their parents don't send them to the streets for a week when they act like brats," Dalva burst out.

Celi, who had been standing by the pizza place's door the whole time while we talked, came over to where Dalva, Lara, and I were and, laughing and talking at the same time, told us that a couple had just given her a bill worth five bucks. It was a lot of money for spare change. "I think they were too drunk to see the bill they were giving me," Celi said, pointing to the couple. We looked at them and, from the way they were walking, wondered whether they were seeing two sidewalks where there was one.

"We have enough money for a *stone* now," Celi said, looking at Dalva.

"Sorry, Tio, we gotta go," Dalva said with an impish smile.

"See you later," I said, wondering where they were going to sleep that night. We kissed goodbye and they left, Lara going with them.

Grace and Kleo were finishing eating when Dalva pointed to a man opening the blue van's door. He threw a large mailbag into the passenger's seat, started the engine, and drove away in a hurry. Kleo and Grace looked at each other and started laughing, stopping only when Dalva began a graphic description of how their smashed bodies would look had they still been sleeping under the van. "You are sick, girl," Grace said to Dalva, and they all began to laugh again. "That's a good way to die anyway, in your sleep—you don't feel anything, just like going to sleep, but you never wake up," Grace said.

"I think so too! It's better than getting shot and left in a ditch to die slowly, like Pedro," Dalva said.

"And Marcy too," Grace recalled.

"You are so gloomy! I don't wanna die young . . . ," Kleo began.

"Get real, girl!" whispered Grace. "How many street kids do you know who live much beyond our age, huh?"

"I'm gonna get off the streets," murmured Kleo, gazing past us.

"Yeah, right! Only if Tio Marcelo here marries you," Grace said, and we all chuckled. Only I blushed.

"Let's go, guys, it's getting late and I want to shower today!" Dalva got up and we followed her lead.

We were two blocks from Casa Aberta, walking through a street market, inebriated by the smells coming from the third-class steaks barbecuing on dozens of grills all around us and from the countless fruit stands stacked with ripe tangerines and guavas, when Dalva abruptly stopped. I stopped too and looked at where Dalva was looking. I saw a woman with black straight hair in a ponytail, wearing jeans and a loose white shirt, only a few steps ahead, staring right back at us.

"It's Regina! Come on, Kleo, hurry up, time to split," Dalva said, pulling Kleo by the hand and running back the way we had come. I didn't even see which way Grace had gone; I just stood there. I figured the woman was the dealer Dalva had told me about. She came up to me and asked for a light. I lit up her cigarette, trying not to shake too much.

"Do you know those little sluts?" the woman said, looking fiercely into my eyes. I was glad that Dalva had seen her in time to escape and that I was in a place with lots of people around.

"I was trying to help them find a place to shower. . . ."

## Developmental Implications

These brief narratives of the street kids' daily lives offer us an avenue for questioning the social and psychological realities in which these youngsters develop and learn about the world. For instance, what effects might the struggle for daily survival on the streets have on cognitive development? How is identity formation affected by a limited experimentation with selves and social roles outside their "little criminals" label?

We cannot measure developmental variables or make generalizing claims based on these stories, but they do tell us that these street kids are forced to focus their energy and attention on the urgency and immediacy of daily survival. Kids have to struggle to get food every time they are hungry, be very imaginative just to bathe, find a different place to sleep every night, and stay away from angry drug dealers and police while nevertheless confined to public spaces. Although their ability to survive under these circumstances shows intelligence and competency in adapting to their immediate environment (Tyler, Tyler, Tommasello, and Connolly, 1992)—Guberman (1996), for example, has shown that Brazilian street children develop mathematical skills for handling money—their extreme focus on the present may further jeopardize other aspects of development already compromised by the absence of supervising and caring adults.

One area of concern is their development of propositional logic. According to Piaget, propositional logic, a system based on abstract and hypothetical reasoning, enables people to weigh the long-term risks and costs of their actions and evaluate the theoretical consequences that their decisions in the present might have in the future. Piagetian theory claims that the development of sophisticated propositional logic requires individuals to be frequently in situations that stimulate abstract and hypothetical reasoning. In the case of kids living on the streets, where the focus on immediate concrete reality is crucial for daily survival, opportunities for development of abstract, long-term reasoning appear to be few. These kids are more likely to act and make decisions based on desires for immediate gratification and egocentric beliefs of invincibility than to rely on hypothetical evaluations of future consequences.

Street kids are already highly exposed to hazardous cultural practices such as drug use, sexual exploitation, and underground activities on a daily basis. Without the sociocognitive conditions necessary to develop systematic use of propositional logic, they are even more likely to engage in these risky activities. For instance, hunger, fear, and peer acceptance, all very concrete immediate realities for these kids, may carry much more weight in the decision to use drugs than the abstract possibilities of respiratory complications or overdose in the future; the need for money or clothes may seem more real in the decision to have sex with strangers than the hypothetical possibility that they might get pregnant or contract a venereal disease; stealing a watch that will give them $5 in exchange, especially when their stomachs are growling or they are craving a drug that will temporarily free them from the depressive consciousness of their condition, will likely outweigh the hypothetical notion of a cold cell in the event that they get caught.

Aggravating this situation is the perception, commonly held and perpetuated by the kids (and society), that they have no future, no room in mainstream social life. So even when propositional reasoning does take place, their future seems already too dreary to be worth caring about. "I know that crack isn't good for me, but I won't live long anyway, so why bother?" Dalva has said on several occasions. Although this reasoning is not developmentally constructive, it is grounded in the reality they know and hence is difficult to challenge. Having already been failed by families and communities under stressful and subhuman conditions, the only governmental intervention they have experienced is repressive police conduct. Even the religious institutions, the self-proclaimed helpers of street kids in Campinas, seem to have been unable to provide more attractive developmental alternatives than the tough streets for many kids. Their only guiding hopes, then, seem to lie in the immediate and concrete rewards of the streets: acceptance among peers (also engaged in activities perceived as "deviant" by society), drug "trips," and the freedom of an unsupervised life.

Identity is another aspect of development that we feel is relevant, for these kids' sense of self is experienced in a particularly unfriendly social context. Unfortunately, little is known about identity formation in kids actually living on the streets. Lucchini (1996a, 1996b), based on samples of Latin American kids working on the streets and kids living in shelters, argues that these kids tend to show shifting identities, claiming membership in different groups, such as family, institution, or street kids, according to varying needs of self-presentation. Nevertheless, he notes a tendency to avoid identification with the street kid image in an attempt to curb stigmatization.

According to George H. Mead (1934), identity, especially at the beginning stages of adolescence, is largely shaped by how others view and interact with an individual and thus is dependent on a dialogical relationship between the individual and his or her social environment. If we accept Mead's perspective, we can imagine how terribly limited street kids in Campinas are in terms of identity formation. They are so often labeled "little criminals" and treated accordingly that they are likely to see the "little criminal" identity as the sole possibility for their being. Every time these kids see themselves represented in the printed and televised media, it is in the context of deviant activities. They are often treated as criminals when they are doing nothing at all or even engaged in honest activity (recall the story about Tate's beating). The names they are called by passersby, police, and even friendly adults are mostly pejorative and associated with deviance. Positive reinforcement and acceptance comes only from other street kids. The labels attached to them by others become a self-fulfilling prophecy, for the typical adolescent questions, "Who am I?" and "What will I become?" are already answered for them by society.

The fact that street kids are often dependent on the goodwill and charity of others (for a coin, a plate of food, or a hand-me-down) is also likely to lower their self-esteem and enhance a sense of inferiority that is carried over to other domains of life (Freire, 1970). For instance, when asked what he would do if he were the mayor of Campinas, Tate said, "Oh, no, I could never be an important person like a mayor! To begin with, who would vote for me if they knew I'd been a street kid?" In spite of the fact that Tate is very smart and seems very self-confident among peers, he appears to have internalized an inferior human condition that can be traced to his identity formation on the street. This internalized inferiority may also come from the extraordinary indifference with which street kids are treated by the general population. Many kids have said that even worse than being yelled at is not being acknowledged, not being answered or looked at when trying to make contact with someone. And this happens far too often not to affect their sense of self.

These kids need opportunities to experiment also with positive identities so that they can believe that it is possible to become more than "little criminals," that they too can become fuller human beings (Freire, 1970). Until these kids start having humanizing encounters with the population, police, social workers, institutions, and media, the future will continue to be a notion too abstract for them to care about or act on. The change in perception from "little criminals" to kids growing up under unacceptable conditions has to occur at many levels of society, from the developers of social policies to volunteers at shelters, from citizens walking the streets of downtown to the juvenile officers trying to maintain order. We hope that the stories presented shed some light on intervention efforts yet to come.

### Note

1. This account is based on field notes collected by Marcelo Diversi during the first seven months of 1996. Names and a few details have been changed to preserve confidentiality. The notes were written in English, translated from interactions in Portuguese.

### References

Aptekar, L. "Street Children in Developing Countries: A Review of Their Conditions." *Cross-Cultural Research*, 1994, *28*, 195–224.

Barker, G., and Knaul, F. "Exploited Entrepreneurs: Street and Working Children in Developing Countries." Working Paper no. 1. New York: Childhope USA, Inc., 1991.

da Silva, R. "Trajetórias de institucionalização de uma geração de ex-menores: O processo de constituição da identidade delinquente em crianças orfãs e abandonadas" [Institutionalization Trajectories of a Generation of Ex-Minors: The Process of Delinquent Identity Formation in Orphaned and Abandoned Children]. Unpublished master's thesis, University of São Paulo, Brazil, 1996.

Denzin, N. *Interpretive Ethnography: Ethnographic Practices for the 21st Century.* Thousand Oaks, Calif.: Sage, 1997.

Denxin, N., and Lincoln, Y. (eds.). *Handbook of Qualitative Research.* Thousand Oaks, Calif.: Sage, 1994.

Freire, P. *Pedagogy of the Oppressed,* trans. Myra Bergman Ramos. (20th anniv. ed.) New York: Continuum, 1970.

Guberman, S. R. "The Development of Everyday Mathematics in Brazilian Children with Limited Formal Education." *Child Development*, 1996, *67*, 1609–1623.

Hatsukami, D., and Fischman, M. "Crack Cocaine and Cocaine Hydrochloride: Are the Differences Myth or Reality?" *Journal of the American Medical Association*, 1996, *276*, 1580–1588.

Jessor, R., Colby, A., and Shweder, R. *Ethnography and Human Development: Context and Meaning in Social Inquiry.* Chicago: University of Chicago Press, 1996.

Lucchini, R. *Sociologie de la survie: L'enfant dans la rue* [Sociology of Survival: Street Children.] Paris: Presses Universitaires de France, 1996a.

Lucchini, R. "The Street and Its Image." *Childhood: A Global Journal of Child Research*, 1996b, *3*, 235–246.

Lusk, M. W. "Street Children of Rio de Janeiro." *International Social Work*, 1992, *35*, 293–305.

Mead, G. H. *Mind, Self and Society: From the Standpoint of a Social Behaviorist.* Chicago: University of Chicago Press, 1934.

Raffaelli, M. "The Family Situation of Street Youth in Latin America: A Cross-National Review." *International Social Work*, 1997, *40*, 89–100.

Richardson, L. *Writing Strategies: Reaching Diverse Audiences.* Thousand Oaks, Calif.: Sage, 1990.

Richardson, L. "Writing: A Method of Inquiry." In N. Denzin and Y. Lincoln (eds.), *Handbook of Qualitative Research.* Thousand Oaks, Calif.: Sage, 1994.

Sanders, T. *Brazilian Street Children: Who They Are.* United Field Service International Report no. 17: Latin America. Indianapolis: United Field Service, 1987.

Steinberg, L. *Adolescence.* (4th ed.) New York: McGraw-Hill, 1996.

Tyler, F., Tyler, S., Tommasello, A., and Connolly, M. "Huckleberry Finn and Street Youth Everywhere: An Approach to Primary Prevention." In G. Albee, L. Bond, and T. Monsey (eds.), *Improving Children's Lives: Global Perspectives on Prevention.* Thousand Oaks, Calif.: Sage, 1992.

UNICEF. *Annual Report.* New York: United Nations, 1989.

MARCELO DIVERSI *received his Ph.D. in Human and Community Development from the University of Illinois at Urbana-Champaign.*

NEY MORAES FILHO *and* MARGARETH MORELLI *are coordinators at the Campinas branch of the National Street Kids' Movement.*

*Although living on the street is an accepted way for Kenyan boys to cope with family poverty, girls are expected to remain at home. Thus girls' presence on the street is more likely to reflect family breakdown and be associated with negative developmental and mental health outcomes.*

# Street Children in Nairobi: Gender Differences in Mental Health

*Lewis Aptekar, Lynda M. Ciano-Federoff*

Two common hypotheses have been advanced about the origins of street children: that modernization leads to a breakdown of families and that street children come from aberrant families who abandon, abuse, or neglect their children. After being accepted in Latin America, these hypotheses were also accepted in Kenya (Dallape, 1987; Kariuki, 1989; Kilbride and Kilbride, 1990; Onyango, Orwa, Ayako, Ojwang, and Kariuki, 1991; Wainaina, 1981). Despite the apparent common sense of these explanations, however, it may well be that only a small percentage of street children come from dysfunctional families. We think this is particularly true if street boys are considered separately from street girls.

In Latin America, particularly Colombia and Brazil, street children have been the focus of research for more than two decades. Most early studies referred to "street children" rather than "street boys" and "street girls." As a result, the differences between the genders were minimized, although there were some notable exceptions (Campos and others, 1994; Raffaelli and others, 1993; Rizzini and Lusk, 1995). The lack of a differential research focus on street boys and street girls is particularly salient in Kenya because girls are more likely to be abandoned and abused than boys (Kabeberi, 1990; Korbin, 1981). Thus if being a street child is the result of neglect or abuse, we would expect a high proportion of girls to be on the streets. As is true in almost all of the underdeveloped countries, however, in Kenya male street children greatly outnumber female street children.

We hypothesized that most Kenyan street boys are taught by their impoverished head-of-household mothers to cope with a very limited economic environment by becoming independent at a far earlier age than the dominant society deems appropriate (Aptekar, Cathey, Ciano, and Giardino, 1995;

Aptekar and Stocklin, 1996). We suspected that an alternate situation exists for street girls. Generally, Kenyan mothers teach girls to cope with the difficulties of poverty by staying at home. Thus if poor girls become street girls, we also hypothesized that, because their presence on the street stems from a breakdown in the family process, they would have more developmental and psychological problems than street boys.

If these hypotheses can be confirmed, the notion that all street children are the products of family dysfunction could be laid aside and explanations of their situation made more gender-specific. Considering that in Kenya nine out of ten street children are male (Onyango, Suda, and Orwa, 1991) and that similar findings come from other places in the developing world (Agnelli, 1986; Aptekar, 1994), these results would lead to a major change not only in understanding the origins of street children but also in perceptions of their psychological functioning. In this chapter, we describe a project funded by the U.S. National Science Foundation to examine how family dynamics relate to the origins of street children, with particular attention given to gender differences.

## The Kenyan Context

Kenya, located on the equator in East Africa, offered ample opportunities to pursue our research question. Kenya's population is composed of Bantu, Nilotic, and Islamic groups that differ considerably in family structure and child-rearing practices (Hakansson, 1994). For example, among some traditional Bantu groups, a divorced woman with children can expect support from her natal family, whereas among some Nilotic groups, such a woman would be forced to fend for herself. There is cross-cultural evidence that child abuse is high in societies where women's opportunities for financial and emotional independence are limited (Korbin, 1981).

If family structures deteriorate due to modernizing pressures, Kenya can also yield information from comparisons of street children from families with varying degrees of modernization. Research indicates that the Kenyan families from which street children emerge are overwhelmingly headed by women (Clark, 1984; Kayongo-Male and Onyango, 1991), nearly 85 percent of whom are unmarried (Onyango, Suda, and Orwa, 1991; Wainaina, 1981). We worked in two of Nairobi's major slums, Kibera and Mathare, to control for the effects of poverty on child rearing while examining gender differences among families with different degrees of traditional culture. We were able to find more traditional cultural practices in Kibera than in Mathare. For example, residents in Kibera were more likely to have extended families involved in child rearing, to have gone through initiation ceremonies, and to identify themselves as belonging to a particular ethnic village in Kibera. In contrast, the Mathare slum was less traditional. Checking the statistics in Muraya's 1993 study of street girls, we found that only 2 percent came from traditional Kibera but more than half came from Mathare. Thus it appeared that modernization was a predicting factor for street girls.

In general, we observed that most Kenyans rarely engaged street children of either gender beyond brief, uncomfortable interactions. From these few encounters and from information received from the sensational stories and images found in the media, we concluded that middle-class Kenyans believe that the problem of street children is epidemic, which has led to considerable inaccuracies about their numbers. For example, in July 1994, the *Daily Nation* reported that there were half a million youth living on Kenyan streets, three hundred thousand of them in Nairobi ("We Will Care for Nairobi's Children"). However, according to an article appearing in the same newspaper two weeks later, the number of street children in Nairobi was thirty thousand ("City Street Children Now 30,000"). In 1991, Undugu, the largest and most experienced group working with street children in Kenya, estimated five to ten thousand street children in Nairobi (Undugu Society of Kenya, 1990–1991). These inconsistencies are reflected by the general public. When we organized focus groups to ascertain the public's opinion of street children, estimates of their number in Nairobi ranged from a thousand to one hundred thousand. When asked to estimate the number of street youth in Kenya, answers ranged from five thousand to a million and a half.

Professional publications present Kenyan street children as a unified, undifferentiated whole, with information broken down by neither gender nor family structure. These publications do, however, depict the children's poverty (Munyakho, 1992). Onyango, Suda, and Orwa (1991) found that 90 percent of street children in Nairobi went to school without anything to eat, 85 percent ate only one meal per day, and fewer than 10 percent of their parents earned more than the equivalent of $20 per month. Suda (1993) found that 75 percent of street children lived in a one-room house with no running water or indoor plumbing. We assumed that poverty was a necessary but not sufficient condition for the origins of Kenyan street children of both genders. We concluded that it is the difference in how families help their male and female children cope with poverty that explains the psychosocial functioning of street children, and this process appears to be gender-specific.

## The Well-Being of Street Children

To get a clearer picture of gender differences in the functioning of street children, we used two methods of data collection: traditional psychological measures and ethnography. Participants in the psychological study were sampled from five programs that served street and working children. The children had different degrees of street experience, ranging from living with neither supervision from parents nor assistance from helping agencies to working on the streets but returning home to families at the end of each working day. Boys were randomly selected from client lists, but it was impossible to get an equal number of randomly selected street girls because there were so few street girls available, so we chose them nonrandomly (as they were made known to us by agencies, researchers, and so on), which tempers the robustness of our conclusions. The sixty-one street children (forty-two male, nineteen female) in the study ranged in age from eight to seventeen ($M = 12.70$ years, $SD = 2.17$). Each child was administered three psychological tests. The Bender-Gestalt (BG) was used to assess neurological functioning. The Draw A Person (DAP) test was used to measure the child's overall emotional well-being to give an idea of the degree of abuse or neglect they might have experienced. Finally, the Raven's Progressive Matrices was used for intellectual assessment. These tests were chosen because they had been successfully used before in cross-cultural contexts, including in Kenya with children of similar ages, as well as with street children in other cultures (Aptekar, 1988, 1994). The tests were translated into Kiswahili and then back-translated into English to verify the accuracy of the translation. All but four children were given the tests in Kiswahili. The tests were scored by Kenyans and Americans who did not have an interest in the outcomes of the study or knowledge about the hypotheses. For more information on the testing, see Aptekar, Cathey, Ciano, and Giardino (1995).

An analysis of variance was performed on each of the measures using gender as the subject variable and controlling for age. Street boys performed significantly better than street girls on the Draw A Person (DAP), Man test, $F$ $(1,45) = 4.13$, $p < .05$. The mean score on the DAP, Man test for street boys was 86.03 ($SD = 14.85$) versus 78.31 ($SD = 11.57$) for street girls. Boys and girls did not differ significantly in intellectual functioning (street boys' score on the Raven's: $M = 29.70$, $SD = 15.87$; street girls' score on the Raven's: $M = 24.79$, $SD = 4.59$), on one test of emotional well-being (street boys' score on the DAP, Woman: $M = 84.33$, $SD = 18.11$; street girls' score on the DAP, Woman: $M = 80.43$, $SD = 11.11$), or on neurological functioning (street boys' score on the BG: $M = 49.97$, $SD = 32.38$; street girls' score on the BG: $M = 69.82$, $SD = 32.92$), all $p > .05$. Thus the hypothesis that street girls would exhibit more psychological maladjustment than boys was only partly supported. Although gender differences on most of these measures were not significant, boys scored in the direction indicating superior functioning on all measures, thus suggesting that further study of these trends is warranted with larger sample sizes.

## Ethnographic Findings

Because of various problems inherent in quantitative testing of street children (see Chapter Five), we also collected ethnographic data. These data were collected by representatives of a variety of disciplines (psychology, anthropology, sociology), ethnic groups (Gusii, Luo, Luhyia, Kamba, Kalenjin, Kikuyu, Meru, Taita), and occupations (an attorney, demographers, a physician, several social scientists, and a group of university students). We also included both current and former street children as researchers. We did this because in ethnography, as in beauty, much of what is seen is in the eye of the beholder.

The ethnographers worked in pairs. For example, one person would ask the child's age, while the other would make an independent estimate of the child's age. Similar procedures were used for comparing the children's stated tribal affiliation with physical characteristics and language skills. The degree of discrepancy noted gave us some idea about the validity of information the children were supplying, and by using this procedure over time, we had some notion of the reliability of the data being collected. We met with the ethnographic data collectors nearly every day to check for problems.

Ethnographers obtained their information from random time samplings, including collecting data during the day and night, during the week and weekends, and in all kinds of weather. We did this to obtain a representative sample of the street children's daily lives. Ethnographic data were also collected during several events and situations, including functions sponsored both for and by street children, when the children were in contact with the police, when the children made a public march en masse to protest the killing of one of their colleagues by a police reservist, and at meetings where the children were asked to talk to representatives from the governmental and nongovernmental programs working with them. These observations provided information not only about street children but also about the public's response to the children.

Before discussing the ethnographic findings, we will present one case study to illustrate the family dynamics and processes. We met Pleasant, the mother of a street child in our study, when she was twenty-eight years of age. By understanding how Pleasant functioned as the head of her impoverished household and coped with both poverty and unstable romantic relationships, it became possible to begin to contextualize the mental health of street children.

At the time of the interview, Pleasant had been married for five years by common law to a night watchman. They had four children (three boys and a girl), whom they supported together until about two years earlier, when her husband began to drift away from the family. This did not come as a surprise to Pleasant: "This is what most men do," she said simply. By the time the husband left home, Pleasant had developed strong ties to other women in her neighborhood who had also been abandoned by their husbands. According to Pleasant, "This is what women do." These women helped each other when necessary, including obtaining food and gaining access to medical care.

By the time Pleasant's oldest son, Mbisa, had his sixth birthday, he was accustomed to playing with older boys in the neighborhood streets. He had plenty of time to practice taking care of himself because his mother rarely supervised his whereabouts. After his father left (and the household income dropped), Mbisa began to drift further from home and go into other neighborhoods to park cars, clean windows, and find other sources of income for his family. Pleasant worked off and on as a domestic servant and showed her daughter, Dominion, how to take care of household chores. By the time Dominion was seven years of age, she would fetch water, make fires, and cook most meals.

While Pleasant and Mbisa both earned income, there was enough money to pay, at least on occasion, school fees for the two younger boys. When Dmisa, a man Pleasant knew from her upcountry community, moved in with Pleasant, their combined incomes not only kept the two younger boys in school for longer periods of time but also allowed Mbisa to return to school.

Pleasant knew the ups and downs of a woman's economic and romantic situation. The fact that her boyfriend would move out (or that she would kick him out) was as expected as the demise in the relationship between herself and her common law husband had been. She knew what the economic implications of these changes would be. Without additional family income, the two younger boys would have to leave school and go work on the streets like Mbisa. However, only complete financial destitution or the utter breakdown of her mental health would result in sending Dominion to the streets. (Some women did have daughters working in the streets, but they would most likely be supervised by an older child, and the mother would make every effort to see that her daughter was not abused.)

Neither Pleasant nor the other women in our study believed they were living in "broken" homes. Many of these women believed they were better off without husbands whom, they reported, were "too expensive to keep in drink, let alone food and clothes." They told us that even if their "husbands" wanted to work, they were unable to find employment. In part this was because of the increasing opportunities in the informal sectors for women and decreasing opportunities in the formal sectors for men. The diary of Maria de Jesus (1962) gives a gripping literary description of how one poor Brazilian woman in a similar situation learned that having men in her house was just too emotionally and economically costly. Peatrie (1968) provides a more scientific account of the same point of view in Venezuela. Similar findings come from a study of family life among the poor in Nairobi, where "40 percent of the mothers . . . felt that marriage spoils a relationship and gives the man too much power and control over the woman" (Suda, 1993, p. 113).

Similar to their mothers, the children in the houses we visited did not view themselves as abandoned when their fathers left, because they had grown up to expect either polygamy or serial partnerships between adult men and women. In addition, we found that most of the children in our study had not experienced the emotional plight that comes from parents dissolving a marriage in a Western-style divorce. Instead these children were accustomed to living in a family that included a series of men staying for short periods of time, some of them more benign than others.

More than three-quarters of the families in our study began with a man and a woman who were not legally married, had children, and later separated. Subsequently, the man and woman formed unions with other partners. As a result, the children eventually belonged to three families: their biological families, their mothers' remarried families (usually common law marriage), and their fathers' remarried families (also common law). In fact, the children in one household might not even come from the same community. Other Kenyan studies point to the same type of family structure (Aptekar, Cathey, Ciano, and Giardino, 1995; Clark, 1984; Njeru, 1994). It has been speculated that this new modern family, unlike the extended traditional family, will not be bound by the sense of common community associated with traditional African kin (Erny, 1981).

There are interpersonal and psychological problems associated with this new family structure that relate to the origins of street children. First, sibling relationships in this type of family become very complex. Although it is less recognized as a cause of the children's move to the streets than the alleged abusive stepfather or absent father, sibling rivalry may account for more children leaving their homes than is commonly thought. We found that this information was obscured in studies that asked children only if family problems caused them to leave home. Children did not understand that "family problems" included problems with siblings; if they were not fighting with their parents, they did not report family problems in their responses. However, when we talked in depth with the children, we discovered that many left home because they were having trouble with their half-brothers or half-sisters.

Another problem is that, because of poverty, children are often forced to sleep in the same bed as their mother and siblings (Onyango and others, 1991) and in the same room as their mothers' partners. For example, the 1990–1991 Undugu report stated that 80 percent of the street girls came from homes with only a single room. A major reason we found that girls left home was because they could no longer sleep without the fear of being violated by a nonrelated man living in the house. According to Onyango, Suda, and Orwa (1991), more than 80 percent of the street girls in Nairobi have been sexually abused. The boys in our study, for their part, believed themselves to be too old to sleep in the same bed with their mothers. They had outgrown what they considered to be childlike behavior. No wonder, since they had plenty of time on the streets, learning the ropes of a wide variety of environments, as well as shouldering the responsibility for earning some income.

## Boys' Adaptation to the Street

During our study of street children, we were impressed particularly by the resourcefulness and loyalty of street boys. We found that street boys rarely began street life before they were five years old, and many were in full control of their lives by ten or twelve. Even though independent and occupied by street life, the boys maintained contact with their families. They also earned sufficient money on the streets to share some of it with their families, developed many friendships, found programs available to serve them, and in many other ways acted like adults. Other aspects of the boys' coping strategies also illustrated their ability to function rationally. For example, the boys were able to maneuver the legal system. Each time they were arrested, they gave authorities a different name, which meant that with each offense they were given the light sentences afforded first offenders. The boys also took advantage of their friendships with *totes,* young men who escort passengers into *matatus* (vanlike public transportation buses) and collect their money, and drivers of the *matatus,* who helped them travel free on public transportation. Indeed, when compared to other poor boys, street boys worked and played in a far larger geographical area (Suda, 1994). In this expanded geographical terrain, the boys were capable of making the many entrepreneurial deals (for example, finding things cheap in one place and selling them dearer in another) that comprised their daily survival, and this took considerable cognitive skills. The street boys were also aware of the importance of making peace with social workers so that their medical needs could be met when they were ill or injured.

## Girls' Adaptation to the Street

Largely as we characterize our sample of street boys as resourceful, we characterize our sample of street girls as victims of society. In contrast to boys, the girls we studied began street life much later, usually not before they were ten years of age. As girls entered puberty, they were perceived (and evaluated) in sexual terms. If they were not considered attractive by men, they were shunned. Thus girls were reduced to two options, either being rejected by other street children or forced into the role of prostitute. In either case, they were perceived as unworthy of care by street boys and middle-class Kenyans.

We present the following story to illustrate the reason we characterize street girls as victims. One evening a female ethnographer and the first author stopped to talk to several street boys who were living at the end of a deserted alley near an open sewer just outside the city center. They lived in two shacks they had constructed from rubble. To enter we had to bend low to pass through the doorway. To our surprise, we found that two of the occupants were female. Jocylyn, who appeared to have just reached puberty, lay covered in rags, a jar of inhalant in her hand. Through glazed eyes, she barely greeted us. We inferred that she didn't need our attention because she was being "protected" by several of the older street boys. The next day, we returned to the site, and thanks to the skill of the female ethnographer (and promises of financial assistance), we were able to take her to a center that serves street girls where she had been treated well before. Presumably because she was cooperating with us and violating the behavioral expectations put on street girls by street boys, upon arrival at the center, none of her peers, some of whom she knew, greeted her.

Over the next several days, we were able to get some idea of Jocylyn's background. Jocylyn had been raised in Mathare by her mother and had three older brothers. When sales of her mother's illegal beer were good, Jocylyn's brothers went to school while Jocylyn stayed at home to help out with chores and business. Because her mother was not always present, she was abused several times by men who came in to buy beer. Her mother, Jocylyn said, "never helped me." Over time, she began to make friends with older boys, one of whom she liked enough to accept his invitation to live with him in the alley. Before long, she was in a similar position as she had been at home. Because many of the boys found her attractive, they paid her friend to enjoy her company. With nowhere to turn, she tried to find refuge in inhalants.

We tried to bring Jocylyn's mother in to help with the situation but could not locate her. We were told that she had been caught by the police and was in prison. We were eventually able to find her, but Jocylyn had returned to the streets by then. Our forays into the alley to find her were met with increasing hostility; once she threw stones at us. The next time we looked for her, we could not gain entry, and we never saw her again.

The path that Jocylyn appeared to be traveling was a common one for street girls. For example, by the time they became young adults, the girls studied by Muraya (1993) and Suda (1994) were following in their mothers' footsteps, having children, often many and by different men. As a rule, the men did not regard them as legitimate wives and therefore deemed the women and children unworthy of continued financial support. Other Kenyan studies corroborate this finding (Clark, 1984; Kilbride and Kilbride, 1990; Nelson, 1978–1979; Suda, 1994).

Our ethnographic data indicated that boys coped with the pressures of street life by congregating in groups with other male street children. The leaders of these groups commonly took on several street girls as "wives." Each boy saw that his "wives" were not bothered by other boys, from inside or outside the group, and that the girls got enough to eat. In return, the boys received the sexual privileges of husbands. Although some of the girls on the streets exchanged sex for money on a limited basis, none of the girls in Muraya's study (1993), the most complete study of Kenyan street girls, supported herself solely by prostitution. Similarly, we found that the "husbands" were content to let their "wives" live with the dual roles of wife and prostitute. Whatever else the street girls were learning in these male groups, they were learning the low status of women, the same status they witnessed as children in the homes of their mothers.

It would have seemed just as developmentally appropriate for the girls to be deeply committed to same-sex friendships in groups as the boys were (see Aptekar, 1988, 1989, on the psychological value of prepubescent street children of both sexes to play with same-gender friends). However, neither we nor Muraya (1993) found a strong unisex group structure among the girls. Many girls seemed to cope only as appendages to boys, even though the boys did not provide the support they needed. Indeed, the very liberty that the boys allowed the girls in their dual roles as "wives" and as sources of income via sexual favors illustrated the lack of care they gave them. Yet the girls accepted this, evidently feeling unable to conceive an alternative possibility.

If, as we assume, boys are expected to bring income into the house, and thus go to the streets to do so, while girls are expected to stay at home and help out with household chores, street boys and street girls will relate to their families of origin differently. Indeed, we found that almost all the street boys in our study remained connected to their mothers; in fact, the boys often contributed part of their income to the parent. (The same is true of street children in Latin

America; see Aptekar, 1988, 1992; Ennew, 1994; Lusk, 1992.) One of the former street boys working on the project, for example, routinely took a three-hour bus trip to give his mother half of what he had earned during the week. This was common knowledge among his peers, and he was given high status for his behavior. In contrast, the girls were not connected to their families of origin. For example, Muraya (1993) found that two-thirds of Nairobi's street girls severed family ties completely. We also found that street boys were eager to make friends with outsiders and establish close sibling-type relationships with other boys. In contrast, street girls remained distant, even after considerable time spent with Kenyan women experienced in working with street girls (including the women working in our study). As mentioned earlier, street girls did not form strong friendships with other girls.

Our ethnographic findings confirmed our hypotheses. We found that many Kenyan girls are raised in female-centered homes, and if they end up on the streets, it is often because they were abused or had conflicts at home. On the streets, the coping strategies of their mothers failed to protect them. Whereas boys are taught by their mothers from an early age to survive on the streets and rummage to supplement the family income, girls do not get such training, which contributes to their vulnerability in this harsh context. Partly as a result of this situation, our findings suggest that girls may suffer from more mental health problems than street boys.

## Conclusions

Street children generally come from homes headed by single mothers. These women have developed a coping strategy that teaches their male children to develop independence at a far faster rate than is assumed to be healthy by middle-class norms. The public regards the children as out of control and in need of help. These views are reinforced and encouraged by the press and by the underfunded programs that must demonstrate to donors that the problem is endemic.

Despite the fact that street children are often referred to generically, the differences between Kenyan street boys and street girls are considerable. The results of the psychological study and the ethnographic data, taken together, suggest that girls on the streets show more evidence of developmental problems and psychological disturbance than boys. Boys were found to be significantly better adjusted than girls on a measure of overall emotional well-being. Because girls are trained to stay at home and learn from their mothers how to become women, girls on the streets represent a broken path of development. They are more likely to be on the streets because they have fled from homes in which they have not been protected. Conversely, boys are more likely to leave home because they have been taught, by economic necessity, to leave. These gender differences suggest a need to rethink how street children are viewed and dealt with.

# References

Agnelli, S. *Street Children: A Growing Urban Tragedy.* London: Weidenfeld & Nicholson, 1986.

Aptekar, L. *Street Children of Cali.* Durham, N.C.: Duke University Press, 1988.

Aptekar, L. "Characteristics of the Street Children of Colombia." *Child Abuse and Neglect,* 1989, *13,* 427–439.

Aptekar, L. "Are Colombian Street Children Neglected? The Contributions of Ethnographic and Ethnohistorical Approaches to the Study of Children." *Anthropology and Education Quarterly,* 1992, *22,* 326–349.

Aptekar, L. "Street Children in the Developing World: A Review of Their Condition." *Cross-Cultural Research,* 1994, *28,* 195–224.

Aptekar, L., Cathey, P. J., Ciano, L. M., and Giardino, G. "Street Children of Nairobi, Kenya." *African Insight,* 1995, *26*(3), 250–259.

Aptekar, L., and Stocklin, D. "Growing Up in Particularly Difficult Circumstances: A Cross-Cultural Perspective." In. J. W. Berry, P. R. Dasen, and T. S. Swaraswathi (eds.), *Handbook of Cross-Cultural Psychology.* Vol. 2: *Basic Processes and Developmental Psychology.* Needham Heights, Mass.: Allyn & Bacon, 1996.

Campos, R., and others. "Social Networks and Daily Activities of Street Youth in Belo Horizonte, Brazil." *Child Development,* 1994, *65,* 319–330.

"City Street Children Now 30,000." *Nairobi Daily Nation,* July 20, 1994, p. 4.

Clark, M. "Women-Headed Households and Poverty: Insights from Kenya." *Signs: Journal of Women in Culture and Society,* 1984, *10,* 338–354.

Dallape, F. *An Experience with Street Children.* Nairobi: Man Graphics, 1987.

de Jesus, M. *Child of the Dark: The Diary of Carolina Maria de Jesus.* New York: Dutton, 1962.

Ennew, J. "Parentless Friends: A Cross-Cultural Examination of Networks Among Street Children and Street Youth." In F. Nestman and K Hurrelman (eds.), *Social Networks and Social Support in Childhood and Adolescence.* London: Aldine de Gruyter, 1994.

Erny, G. *The Child and His Environment in Black Africa: An Essay on Traditional Education.* Nairobi: Oxford University Press, 1981.

Hakansson, N. T. "The Detachability of Women: Gender and Kinship in Processes of Socio-Economic Change Among the Gusii of Kenya." *American Ethnologist,* 1994, *21,* 516–538.

Kabeberi, J. *Child Custody, Care and Maintenance.* Nairobi: Oxford University Press, 1990.

Kariuki, P. "In Search of a Sense of Identity: Coping with Single Parenthood in Kenya." *Early Child Development and Care,* 1989, *50,* 25–30.

Kayongo-Male, D., and Onyango, P. *The Sociology of the African Family.* London: Longman, 1991.

Kilbride, P., and Kilbride, J. *Changing Family Life in East Africa: Women and Children at Risk.* University Park: Pennsylvania State University Press, 1990.

Korbin, J. *Child Abuse and Neglect: Cross-Cultural Perspectives.* Berkeley: University of California Press, 1981.

Lusk, M. "Street Children of Rio de Janeiro." *International Social Work,* 1992, *35,* 293–305.

Munyakho, D. *Kenya: Child Newcomers to the Urban Jungle.* New York: UNICEF, 1992.

Muraya, J. *Street Children: A Study of Street Girls in Nairobi, Kenya.* Swansea, Wales: Center for Development Studies, University College of Swansea, 1993.

Nelson, N. "Female-Centered Families: Changing Patterns of Marriage and Family Among Buzaa Brewers of Mathare Valley." *African Urban Studies,* 1978–1979, *3,* 85–104.

Njeru, E. "Nairobi Street Children Study: Socioeconomic Area Profiles." Unpublished manuscript, University of Nairobi, 1994.

Onyango, P., Suda, C., and Orwa, K. *A Report on the Nairobi Case Study on Children in Especially Difficult Circumstances.* Florence, Italy: UNICEF, 1991.

Onyango, P., and others. *A Summary of a Study of Street Children in Kenya.* Nairobi: African Network for the Prevention and Protection Against Child Abuse and Neglect, 1991.

Peatrie, L. *The View from the Barrio.* Ann Arbor: University of Michigan Press, 1968.
Raffaelli, M., and others. "Sexual Practices and Attitudes of Street Youth in Belo Horizonte, Brazil." *Social Science and Medicine,* 1993, *37,* 661–670.
Rizzini, I., and Lusk, M. "Children in the Streets: Latin America's Lost Generation." *Children and Youth Services Review,* 1995, *17,* 391–400.
Suda, C. "The Impact of Changing Family Structures on Nairobi Children." *African Study Monographs,* 1993, *14,* 109–121.
Suda, C. *Report of a Baseline Survey on Street Children in Nairobi.* Nairobi: Institute of African Studies, University of Nairobi, 1994.
Undugu Society of Kenya. *Experiences in Community Development.* Nairobi: Undugu Society of Kenya, 1990–1991.
Wainaina, J. "The 'Parking Boys' of Nairobi." *African Journal of Sociology,* 1981, *1,* 7–45.
"We Will Care for Nairobi's Children." *Nairobi Daily Nation,* July 6, 1994, p.4.

LEWIS APTEKAR *is a professor of counseling psychology at San Jose State University.*

LYNDA M. CIANO-FEDEROFF *is a graduate student in clinical psychology at West Virginia University.*

*In the United States, family dysfunction is a major precipitant for adolescents to leave home and puts many youth at risk even before they run away to the streets. The resulting alienation from family and society jeopardizes these youths' chances of making a successful transition to adulthood.*

# Homeless Youth in the United States: Description and Developmental Issues

*Jacqueline Smollar*

Homeless youth in the United States are defined as individuals under nineteen years of age who meet at least one of the following criteria:

- They have run away from their homes or from their alternative care placements and remained away for a long period of time with little or no connection with their families or caretakers.
- They have been pushed out of their homes or foster care placements, have been abandoned by their parents, or have left home for the streets with their parents' knowledge and consent.
- They have no stable place of residence; lack adult supervision, guidance, and care; and have little likelihood of reunification with parents.

The current number of homeless youth in the United States is not known; estimates range from one hundred thousand to five hundred thousand (Dietz and Coburn, 1991). Although estimates of one to two million (Office of the Inspector General, 1983; Williams, 1984) have appeared in the literature, these larger estimates include youth who run away from home and return fairly quickly, usually within a few days (Adams, Gullotta, and Clancy, 1985).

Homeless youth reside in environments that often differ considerably from those of their peers who reside with families or in alternative care placements. The kinds of environments in which these adolescents spend their teenage years may have a significant impact on their developmental outcomes. This chapter examines the developmental implications of youth homelessness and discusses the history of youth homelessness in the United States and the characteristics of homeless youth and their families.

New Directions for Child and Adolescent Development, no. 85, Fall 1999 © Jossey-Bass Publishers

## The Changing Face of Homeless Youth in the United States

Homeless youth have been a part of U.S. society since its early history. During the settlement of the original thirteen colonies and the ensuing era of westward expansion, many adolescents left home to seek adventure and economic opportunity (Libertoff, 1980).

Homeless youth were also prevalent in the 1800s, particularly in large urban areas. They were perceived, however, not as adventure seekers but as criminals constituting a significant social problem. In 1820, a newspaper published the following comments of a New York City police chief (in Libertoff, 1980, p. 152):

> I allude to the constantly increasing numbers of vagrant, idle and vicious children of both sexes, who infest our public fares, hotels, docks. . . . Wherever their inclination leads them, a large proportion of these juvenile vagrants are in the daily practice of pilfering whatever offers and begging where they cannot steal. The female portion of the youngest class, those who have only seen some eight or twelve summers, are addicted to immoralities of the most loathsome description.

These youth were from poor immigrant families and were neither wanted nor needed in the labor force (Libertoff, 1980). Social workers at the time frequently interceded on behalf of these youth, believing that they could be reformed given the right circumstances (Rothman, 1991). This belief led to the establishment of "houses of refuge," later known as reform schools, designed to provide youth with environments conducive to positive social development (Rothman, 1991).

Many youth became homeless during the Great Depression years, again due primarily to poverty and the absence of employment opportunities (Libertoff, 1980). However, because large segments of the population were homeless during that era, the specific problem of youth homelessness was generally ignored.

In the 1960s, a new group of homeless youth, referred to as "runaways," began to be perceived as a significant social problem. Unlike homeless youth of the 1800s and the Great Depression, these adolescents left middle- and upper-class homes and forfeited the educational advantages and future professional prospects available to them as part of their families' socioeconomic status (Libertoff, 1980). Running away in the 1960s was generally attributed to the influence of the youth culture, which encouraged young people to reject their parents' values and engage in activities that fostered self-exploration and self-expression (Libertoff, 1980).

Regardless of their reasons for running away, these youth were at considerable risk for being victimized by adults, who involved them in drug dealing, prostitution, child pornography, and other criminal activities. Consequently, Congress enacted the Runaway Youth Act of 1974, which described runaway youth as being at high risk for severe physical and psychological damage and provided funds for establishing shelters to house the youth temporarily and reunite them with their parents. To ensure rapid reunification, shelter staff were required to inform parents or legal guardians of a youth's presence in the shelter within forty-eight hours of arrival, and the shelters could not house anyone longer than fourteen days except under special circumstances.

The Runway Youth Act was revised in 1977 and renamed the Runaway and Homeless Youth Act. The 1977 act was a response to reports from youth shelter personnel that they were seeing many young people who had not run away from home but had been pushed out of their homes, been abandoned by parents, or left home for life on the street with their parents' knowledge and consent (Lourie, Campiglia, James, and Dewitt, 1979; U.S. Senate, 1980). The act made funds available to expand the number of shelters and types of services. Although the act continued to stress family reunification, it acknowledged that both youth and their families needed extensive services for reunifications to be successfully accomplished.

The number of teens seen by the shelter system who had not run away from home but had been pushed out or abandoned or remained away with parental consent continued to increase during the 1980s. Shelter personnel reported that these young people exhibited multiple psychological and behavioral problems and came from families characterized by parental substance abuse, family violence, child maltreatment, long-term family conflict, and dysfunctional parents, many of whom had severe psychological and behavioral problems (Kufeldt and Nimmo, 1987; Kurtz, Kurtz, and Jarvis, 1991; Luna, 1987; Powers, Eckenrode, and Jaklitsch, 1990; Smollar, Youniss, and Ooms, 1986).

In the 1990s, family dysfunction continued to be a primary cause of youth homelessness, although poverty once again emerged as a potential contributing factor. For example, in two studies conducted in the 1980s, one found that only 10 percent of a sample of homeless youth came from families receiving public assistance (Kurtz, 1987), and the other reported that 11 percent of homeless youth seen in shelters came from families in which unemployment was a problem (General Accounting Office, 1989). In contrast, two studies conducted in the 1990s revealed a much larger percentage of youth from impoverished families. One study found that 40 percent of youth in both a shelter and a street youth sample were from families receiving public assistance or living in publicly assisted housing (Research Triangle Institute, 1995). The other study reported that 41 percent of youth seen in the shelters were from families with long-term economic problems (National Association of Social Workers, 1991). The 1990s also saw an increase in the numbers of youth who were homeless as a result of their families' homelessness (National Coalition for the Homeless, 1997).

From a historical perspective, then, the profile of homeless youth has changed from young people seeking adventure and economic opportunity during the early days of America's growth to those in the nineteenth and early twentieth centuries who were homeless because of poverty, then to the adventure-seeking and rebellious youth of the 1960s, and finally to the troubled youth from dysfunctional families of the final three decades of the century. Family poverty has also reappeared in recent years as a significant characteristic of the homeless youth population.

## The Current Population of Homeless Youth

Accurate knowledge about homeless adolescents is limited by the fact that most studies focus on young people who are seen by the shelter system, which is only a small percentage of the total number of homeless youth. One report estimated that only one in twelve homeless youth ever comes into contact with the shelter system (Office of the Inspector General, 1983). A few studies have focused on "street youth"—teens who do not have a permanent residence, usually spend their days on the streets, and are without adult supervision. However, these studies usually assess the risks that youth encounter as a result of living on the streets rather than their characteristics or their reasons for leaving home. Despite these limitations, there is sufficient research to draw some general conclusions about the causes of youth homelessness, the characteristics of homeless youth, and the nature of life on the streets.

The primary cause of youth homelessness is family dysfunction, specifically parental neglect, physical or sexual abuse, family substance abuse, and family violence (Adams, Gullota, and Clancy, 1985; Farber and Joseph, 1985; General Accounting Office, 1989; Janus, McCormack, Burgess, and Hartman, 1987; Kurtz, Kurtz, and Jarvis, 1991; Luna, 1987; National Association of Social Workers, 1991; Powers, Eckenrode, and Jaklitsch, 1990; Research Triangle Institute, 1995). Furthermore, these family problems have been found to be long-standing ones, rather than single episodes occurring shortly before youth leave home (Kurtz, Kurtz, and Jarvis, 1991; Powers, Eckenrode, and Jaklitsch, 1990).

Given their home environments, it is not surprising that homeless youth exhibit multiple personality and behavioral problems prior to leaving home (Fors and Rojek, 1991; Research Triangle Institute, 1995). These include poor coping skills, suicidal tendencies, school failure or underachievement, mental health problems, depression, substance abuse, and a history of having been in alternative care placements, juvenile justice facilities, or psychiatric hospitals.

Homeless youth lead unstable and hazardous lives (Kearon, 1989; Luna, 1991; Young, Godfrey, Matthews, and Adams, 1983). They rarely reside in one location for long, and many have been found to live in four or more places over a six-month period (Lucas and Hackett, 1995). Homeless youth are at high risk for health problems, particularly hepatitis, respiratory problems (asthma and pneumonia), scabies, and trauma (Forst and Blomquist, 1991). They exhibit high levels of depression, suicidal tendencies, and suicide attempts (Kruks, 1991; Smart and Walsh, 1993), although one study reported that the incidence of suicide attempts was higher prior to leaving home than after leaving (Research Triangle Institute, 1995). Homeless youth also exhibit poor mental health, high use of alcohol and other drugs, and high risk factors for contracting HIV (Athey, 1991; Greene, Ennett, and Ringwalt, 1997; Luna, 1991).

Homeless youth who are homosexual have been found to have a greater and more severe incidence of problems such as depression and suicide than other homeless youth. In one study of homeless street youth, 53 percent of homosexual adolescents had attempted suicide, compared to 32 percent of a cohort that did not differentiate individuals by sexual orientation (Kruks, 1991). Similarly, homeless youth on the streets who use drugs and alcohol tend to experience more severe consequences than those who do not use, although the latter comprise a very small group. For example, those who were substance abusers reported being robbed, attacked, sexually victimized, and engaging in prostitution more often than those who were not substance abusers (Lucas and Hackett, 1995).

These research findings suggest that homeless youth reside in high-risk environments both before and after they leave home. While homeless, their incidence of substance abuse, addiction, prostitution, and other criminal activities as well as their poor health status suggests that many of them will not survive until adulthood without significant interventions, although there are no statistics at present on the numbers that do not survive. Those that do not die or contract terminal diseases are still at risk of never becoming productive members of adult society. For example, one study has found that homelessness during adolescence is a significant predictor of adult homelessness (Simons and Whitbeck, 1991).

Although the developmental implications of youth homelessness in the United States have not been examined directly, the research on developmental processes during adolescence may be used to understand the consequences of youth homelessness. The results of this research and their implications for developmental outcomes among homeless youth may serve to guide future program, research, and policy initiatives directed toward this population.

## Adolescent Development and Homeless Youth

Development is a process that occurs through reciprocal and dynamic interactions that take place between individuals and various aspects of their environment, with the person and the environment simultaneously influencing one another. Through examining the individual and environmental characteristics that foster positive development among adolescents, it is possible to draw inferences about the developmental prospects for homeless youth.

Four specific characteristics that foster positive developmental pathways from childhood to adulthood have been identified (CSR, Inc., 1997):

• A sense of industry and competency
• A feeling of connectedness to others and to society

- A sense of control over one's fate in life
- A stable sense of identity

These characteristics are associated with positive school performance, prosocial behavior during adolescence, membership in nondeviant peer groups, and positive relationships with parents and peers (Cairns and Cairns, 1994; Werner and Smith, 1992). These characteristics and the environmental interactions that foster their development are discussed in the following sections with regard to homeless youth.

**A Sense of Industry and Competency.** Individuals who are confident in their own abilities develop a sense of industry and competency. Being involved in productive activities in school, at home, or in the community, and winning recognition for this productivity, nurtures this sense of industry and competency in children. This in turn fosters the development of a stable identity during adolescence and the perception of oneself as a potentially productive member of society (Erikson, 1968).

Youth who become homeless do not appear to have the opportunity to engage in interactions and activities that foster the development of a sense of industry or competency in their school environments. American homeless youth have been found to have a history of school failure that often dates back to their early school years (Nye, 1980; Research Triangle Institute, 1995). They exhibit poor attitudes toward schooling, behavior problems in school, and a history of conflicts with teachers (Gutierres and Reich, 1981; Nye, 1980). One study of homeless youth (Kurtz, Kurtz, and Jarvis, 1991) reported that prior to leaving home, about 40 percent of the youth did not attend school regularly, either due to being truant, suspended, or expelled or having dropped out entirely. Another study (Kurtz, 1987) found that only 44 percent of a sample of homeless youth had attended school regularly before leaving home, 43 percent had failed or repeated a grade in school, and 11 percent had failed more than once.

The home environments of homeless youth also do not appear to provide many opportunities for developing a sense of industry or competency. While living at home or in foster care placements, these youth reported that their parents or caretakers constantly denigrated them, frequently expressed dissatisfaction with them, and spent very little time with them (Adams, Gullotta, and Clancy, 1985; Spillane-Grieco, 1984).

Once they are homeless, many youth have the opportunity to experience a sense of industry and competency, often for the first time in their lives. Youth who quickly develop the survival skills necessary for life on the streets find that they are able to win recognition from other homeless youth and adults in the street culture who value those skills (Luna, 1989; Orten and Soll, 1980). However, because these skills often include shoplifting, stealing, swindling, pickpocketing, prostitution, and begging, they are not consistent with skills valued by mainstream American society. Consequently, the sense of competency developed in the context of the street culture may further impede the potential of these individuals for becoming integrated into mainstream society. In fact, youth services professionals have reported that the most difficult youth to reach with services are often those who have achieved the greatest success in adapting to street life (Luna, 1987; Smollar, Youniss, and Ooms, 1986).

**A Feeling of Connectedness to Others.** Interactions that promote development of a sense of connectedness to other people are those in which adults provide social and emotional support to adolescents while permitting them psychological and emotional independence (Barber, Olsen, and Shagle, 1995; Youniss and Smollar, 1985). Interactions in which adults attempt to control adolescents' behaviors by monitoring their activities and applying sanctions in a consistent and caring manner also promote the development of a sense of connectedness because they signal to adolescents that adults in the family or community care about them and are willing to become involved in their lives (Patterson and Dishion, 1985; Sampson and Laub, 1994).

Research on the family lives of American homeless youth prior to leaving home suggests that these individuals have few opportunities to develop a sense of connectedness to parents. As noted previously, most homeless teens are leaving homes in which they were abused or neglected rather than supported or encouraged. In one study, it was found that 60 percent of youth in shelters nationwide were physically or sexually abused by parents (National Association of Social Workers, 1991). Furthermore, the parents of homeless youth, rather than monitoring them in a caring and consistent manner, were found to be excessively strict, use excessive punishment, or be highly neglectful (Adams, Gullotta, and Clancy, 1985).

The incidence of physical and sexual abuse experienced by these youth suggests that their interactions with parents are more likely to promote a sense of alienation from others and from society rather than a sense of connectedness. Physical and sexual abuse have been found to have long-term and devastating effects on youth development and self-esteem and to increase overall behavior problems (Stiffman, 1989). The lack of connectedness between maltreated homeless youth and their families is evident in the fact that parents often knew that their children were leaving home and informed shelter personnel that they did not want their children to return home (Kurtz, Kurtz, and Jarvis, 1991).

Some researchers have suggested that one of the reasons why many of these children leave home is to find the connectedness that is missing in their lives—the love and support they did not get at home (Luna, 1987; Spillane-Grieco, 1984). In fact, many homeless youth report that they were able to find adults who cared about them while living on the streets (Luna, 1987, 1991). Unfortunately, these adults often exploited them and involved them in criminal activities. Searching for connectedness may make many homeless youth particularly vulnerable to exploitation by adults.

While on the streets, homeless youth also appear to develop a strong sense of connectedness to one another, which offers them a semblance of security and comfort. Street companions often provide the friendship, acceptance, and understanding previously lacking at home or in foster care placements (Luna, 1987). As difficult as life is on the streets, many homeless youth prefer it to the homes they left (Rader, 1982).

Although homeless youth may be able to develop a sense of connectedness to other persons, they are not developing a sense of connectedness to society. As a result of years of victimization by parents or other caretakers, homeless youth are mistrustful and fearful of society's institutions and do not believe that these institutions are concerned about their welfare. For that reason, homeless youth typically have not made use of traditional services and community resources. Shelter personnel frequently report that the most difficult task in working with street youth is gaining their trust (Beatty and Carlson, 1985; Shore, 1986).

**A Sense of Control over One's Fate in Life.** Adolescents who have a sense of control over their fate believe that they have some influence over what happens to them. This belief appears to be nurtured when from an early age children are engaged in interactions in which they can successfully predict the outcomes of their actions. When parents or other adults consistently respond to prosocial behaviors with positive sanctions and to misbehaviors with negative sanctions, children learn that their behaviors are related to particular responses (Patterson and Dishion, 1985; Sampson and Laub, 1994).

The dysfunctional families of many homeless youth in the United States do not provide the kind of consistent and contingent responses that promote the development of a sense of control over one's fate in life. Parental substance abuse and family violence often result in parent-child interactions characterized by random responses to children's behaviors. Consequently, children in these families are likely to develop a sense of helplessness rather than control. For many of these youth, leaving home may be a means of trying to gain some control over their fate in life. However, life on the streets does not appear to provide these youth with many opportunities to engage in interactions that foster the development of a sense of control over their lives.

**Sense of Identity.** Development of a stable identity has been found to be associated with positive interpersonal relationships, psychological and behavioral stability, and productive adulthood (Grotevant, 1996). The development of a stable identity is derived from an adolescent's sense of competency, connectedness to others and to the larger society, and control (CSR, Inc., 1997). As noted earlier, homeless youth are unlikely to have opportunities to engage in interactions that foster the development of these characteristics prior to leaving their homes. Consequently, they are unlikely to have formed the basis for a stable identity before becoming homeless.

The fact that some homeless youth are able to develop a sense of competency with respect to survival skills on the streets and connectedness to others in their street communities may provide a basis for identity development. However, the identity that develops out of this process is likely to reflect alienation from society and identification with the street culture (Miller, Eggertson-

Tacon, and Quigg, 1990) and hence would not be likely to foster productive adulthood.

## Implications for Social Policies and Services for Homeless Youth

Because homeless youth in the United States tend to come from severely dysfunctional families, they are already at risk for negative developmental outcomes prior to running away. Although leaving home may be an adaptive response to a threatening situation, those who leave to escape serious family problems often face equally threatening problems on the street.

The prospects for homeless youth making a successful transition from childhood to adulthood are not positive. These youth do not have families that offer guidance, structure, and encouragement; they are isolated from the institutions of society; and although they often develop a sense of connectedness to the street community, that community generally does not provide the assistance and support necessary to foster positive developmental pathways.

One implication for social policies and services is that homeless youth need not only safe places to live, access to education and job training, and physical and mental health services but also environments in which they can engage in interactions with adults and peers that are productive of positive developmental pathways. Although the North American youth shelter system offers these kinds of environmental opportunities, the efforts of this system are often impeded by the short time period in which youth can remain in the shelter and by the scarcity of long-term care options for youth. The U.S. government's focus on reunification with families needs to be rethought in the light of the evidence that many of these youth do not have families to which they can return, and many of the families they could return to are likely to be highly dysfunctional (Shore, 1986; National Network of Runaway and Youth Services, 1988).

Altering the developmental pathways or outcomes of homeless youth is not an easy task. A major challenge is that only a small percentage of homeless youth seek assistance from the community agencies that have been established to help them. This suggests that more outreach is needed to contact these youth and provide the services that they need.

Another challenge to helping homeless youth develop along more positive pathways is the absence of advocacy efforts for youth among North American professional organizations. Developmentalists, long active in advocating services for young children, have not made the same effort on behalf of adolescents. Homeless youth need greater access to care facilities or family homes that offer opportunities for developmentally productive interactions, and youth services professionals need access to information about what types of interventions are effective with this population. Increased advocacy, as well as increased research efforts by professionals and their organizations, would foster services to help homeless youth develop along more positive pathways.

# References

Adams, G., Gullotta, T., and Clancy, M. "Homeless Adolescents: A Descriptive Study of Similarities and Differences Between Runaways and Throwaways." *Adolescence,* 1985, *20,* 715–724.

Athey, J. L. "HIV Infection and Homeless Adolescents." *Child Welfare,* 1991, *70,* 517–528.

Barber, B. K., Olsen, J. E., and Shagle, S. C. "Associations Between Parental Psychological and Behavioral Control and Youth Internalized and Externalized Behaviors." *Child Development,* 1995, *65,* 1120–1136.

Beatty, J. W., and Carlson, H. M. "Street Kids: Children in Danger." Paper presented at the meetings of the American Psychological Association, Los Angeles, 1985.

Cairns, R. B., and Cairns, B. D. *Lifelines and Risks: Pathways of Youth in Our Time.* New York: Cambridge University Press, 1994.

CSR, Inc. *Understanding Youth Development: Promoting Positive Pathways of Growth.* Report prepared for the U.S. Department of Health and Human Services, Family and Youth Services Bureau, 1997.

Dietz, P., and Coburn, J. *To Whom Do They Belong? Runaway, Homeless, and Other Youth in High-Risk Situations in the 1990s.* Washington, D.C.: National Network for Runaway and Youth Services, 1991.

Erikson, E. *Identity: Youth and Crisis.* New York: Norton, 1968.

Farber, E., and Joseph, J. "The Maltreated Adolescent: Patterns of Physical Abuse." *Child Abuse and Neglect,* 1985, *9,* 201–206.

Fors, S. W., and Rojek, D. G. "A Comparison of Drug Involvement Between Runaways and School Youths." *Journal of Drug Education,* 1991, *21,* 13–25.

Forst, M. L., and Blomquist, M. E. *Missing Children.* San Francisco: New Lexington Press, 1991.

General Accounting Office. *Homelessness: Homeless and Runaway Youth Receiving Services at Federally Funded Shelters.* Report to the Honorable Paul Simon, U.S. Senate, 1989.

Greene, J. M., Ennett, S. T., and Ringwalt, C. L. "Substance Use Among Runaway and Homeless Youth in Three National Samples." *American Journal of Public Health,* 1997, *87,* 229–235.

Grotevant, H. D. "Adolescent Development in Family Contexts." In W. Damon and N. Eisenberg (eds.), *Handbook of Child Psychology.* Vol. 3: *Social Emotional and Personality Development.* (5th ed.) New York: Wiley, 1996.

Gutierres, S. E., and Reich, J. W. "A Developmental Perspective on Runaway Behavior: Its Relationship to Child Abuse." *Child Welfare,* 1981, *60,* 89–94.

Janus, M., McCormack, A., Burgess, A. W., and Hartman, C. *Adolescent Runaways: Course and Consequences.* San Francisco: New Lexington Press, 1987.

Kearon, W. G. "Deinstitutionalization and Abuse of Children on Our Streets." *Juvenile and Family Court Journal,* 1989, *40,* 21–26.

Kruks, G. "Gay and Lesbian Homeless/Street Youth: Special Issues and Concerns." *Journal of Adolescent Health,* 1991, *12,* 515–518.

Kufeldt, K., and Nimmo, M. "Youth on the Street: Abuse and Neglect in the Eighties." *Child Abuse and Neglect,* 1987, *11,* 531–543.

Kurtz, P. D. *Profile: Maltreated Runaway Youth.* Report to the Southeastern Network of Youth and Family Services, Inc., Athens, Ga., 1987.

Kurtz, P. D., Kurtz, G. L., and Jarvis, S. V. "Problems of Maltreated Runaway Youth." *Adolescence,* 1991, *26,* 543–552.

Libertoff, K. "The Runaway Child in America: A Social History." *Journal of Family Issues,* 1980, *1,* 151–164.

Lourie, I. S., Campiglia, P., James, L. R., and Dewitt, J. "Adolescent Abuse and Neglect: The Role of Runaway Youth Programs." *Children Today,* 1979, *8,* 27–29.

Lucas, B., and Hackett, L. *Street Youth: On Their Own in Indianapolis.* Report prepared for the Health Foundation of Greater Indianapolis, 1995.

Luna, G. C. "Welcome to My Nightmare: The Graffiti of Homeless Youth." *Society,* 1987, *24,* 73–78.

Luna, G. C. "Street Youth: Adaptation and Survival in the AIDS Decade." *Journal of Adolescent Health,* 1991, *12,* 511–514.

Miller, A. T., Eggertson-Tacon, C., and Quigg, B. "Patterns of Runaway Behavior Within a Larger Systems Context: The Road to Empowerment." *Adolescence,* 1990, *25,* 271–283.

National Association of Social Workers. *Findings from a National Survey of Shelters for Runaway and Homeless Youth.* Washington, D.C.: National Association of Social Workers, 1991.

National Coalition for the Homeless. *Education of Homeless Children and Youth.* NCH Fact Sheet No. 10. Washington, D.C.: National Coalition for the Homeless, 1997.

National Network of Runaway and Youth Services. *Network News,* Winter 1988 [newsletter].

Nye, F. I. "A Theoretical Perspective on Running Away." *Journal of Family Issues,* 1980, *1,* 274–299.

Office of the Inspector General. *National Program Inspection: Runaway and Homeless Youth.* Report to the secretary of the Department of Health and Human Services, Washington, D.C., 1983.

Orten, J. D., and Soll, S. K. "Runaway Children and Their Families." *Journal of Family Issues,* 1980, *1,* 249–261.

Patterson, G., and Dishion, T. "Contribution of Families and Peers to Delinquency." *Criminology,* 1985, *23,* 63–79.

Powers, J. L., Eckenrode, J., and Jaklitsch, B. "Maltreatment Among Runaway and Homeless Youth." *Child Abuse and Neglect,* 1990, *14,* 87–98.

Rader, D. "Who Will Help the Children?" *Parade,* Sept. 5, 1982.

Research Triangle Institute. *Youth with Runaway, Thrownaway, and Homeless Experiences: Prevalence, Drug Use, and Other At-Risk Behaviors.* Report to the Administration on Children, Youth and Families, Washington, D.C., 1995.

Rothman, J. *Runaway and Homeless Youth: Strengthening Services to Families and Children.* New York: Longman, 1991.

Sampson, R. J., and Laub, J. H. "Urban Poverty and the Family Context of Delinquency: A New Look at Structure and Process in a Classic Study." *Child Development,* 1994, *65,* 523–540.

Shore, D. *Background Report on Services to Runaway and Homeless Youth.* Report to the Washington, D.C., Alliance Project Task Force, 1986.

Simons, R. L., and Whitbeck, L. B. "Running Away During Adolescence as a Precursor to Adult Homelessness." *Social Service Review,* 1991, *65,* 224–247.

Smart, R. G., and Walsh, G. W. "Predictors of Depression in Street Youth." *Adolescence,* 1993, *28,* 41–50.

Smollar, J., Youniss, J., and Ooms, T. *Family Relationships of Adolescents in Crisis: An Assessment of Research and Programs.* Report prepared for the Department of Health and Human Services, Assistant Secretary's Office of Policy and Evaluation, 1986.

Spillane-Grieco, E. "Characteristics of a Helpful Relationship: A Study of Empathic Understanding and Positive Regard Between Runaways and Their Parents." *Adolescence,* 1984, *19,* 63–75.

Stiffman, A. R. "Physical and Sexual Abuse in Runaway Youths." *Child Abuse and Neglect,* 1989, *13,* 417–426.

U.S. Senate. *Homeless Youth: The Saga of Pushouts and Throwaways in America.* Report of the Committee on the Judiciary, 1980.

Werner, E. E., and Smith, R. S. *Overcoming the Odds: High-Risk Children from Birth to Adulthood.* Ithaca, N.Y.: Cornell University Press, 1992.

Williams, R. "One More Try." *Foundation News,* 1984, *25,* 16–21.

Young, R., Godfrey, W., Matthews, B., and Adams, G. "Runaways: A Review of Negative Consequences." *Family Relations,* 1983, *32,* 275–281.

Youniss, J., and Smollar, J. *Adolescents' Relations with Mothers, Fathers, and Friends.* Chicago: University of Chicago Press, 1985.

JACQUELINE SMOLLAR, *Ph.D., is an independent consultant in the areas of runaway and homeless youth, child abuse and neglect, foster care, early childhood education, and substance abuse.*

*Research with street children raises unique methodological and ethical issues. Drawing on their experience as university-based researchers, the authors offer suggestions for doing research with this difficult-to-study population.*

# Methodological and Ethical Issues in Research with Street Children

*Claudio S. Hutz, Sílvia H. Koller*

The study of street children presents researchers with challenges and difficulties that can hardly be overstated. In this chapter, we address several issues relating to research with this population. First we consider issues of definition and sampling and discuss the confusion that has resulted from lack of definitional clarity or consideration of sample limitations. Then we turn to measurement issues, discussing specific methodological challenges involved in collecting data from street children. Next we address the question of how to approach street children, focusing particularly on researcher training. We end with a discussion of some of the ethical concerns inherent in research with street children and share our thoughts on the responsibilities of researchers who choose to study this population.

Although our discussion in this chapter can be applied to various groups of children living and developing under difficult circumstances, our examples come primarily from our own work at the Center for Psychological Studies on Street Children at the Federal University of Rio Grande do Sul, Brazil. For several years, we have been trying to integrate and apply basic knowledge from developmental and social psychology to improve the quality of life of at-risk populations. One of our main concerns is to ensure that our research has social relevance. That is, we believe that research must benefit the participants and provide knowledge that can be used by communities.

## Definition and Sampling

The first step in any research project is deciding whom to study and determining how to obtain a representative sample. The definition of street children plays a pivotal role in research and may be a significant source of disagreement and confusion about the results of research studies (Koller and Hutz, 1996). The challenge of obtaining a representative sample of street children is also considerable.

**Defining the Population: Who Is a Street Child?**  Children and adolescents who look like drifters can be found on the streets of most large cities in developing countries. These youngsters wear shabby, dirty clothing and can be seen begging, performing menial chores, working, or just wandering apparently without a purpose. They share an appearance of abandonment that may lead researchers to single them out as street children. However, although these children look alike, they have different family characteristics, life histories, and prognoses. Some scholars believe that the expression "street children" is in itself problematic, giving a distorted message because of an implicit assumption that these children are alike (Dallape, 1996), that they live on the streets in the same way and for similar reasons (Felsman, 1985). In recognition of this, researchers have attempted to divide their samples into subgroups that differ on key characteristics. However, this is not always done in a consistent manner.

Researchers have attempted to classify samples of street children in many different ways. The broadest categorizations divide children into two groups: *children of the streets* and *children in the streets* (for example, Barker and Knaul, 1991; Campos and others, 1994). Children *of* the streets are those who actually live on the street and do not have stable family ties. In contrast, children *in* the streets live with their families and may attend school but spend all or part of their time on the streets, trying to make money for themselves or their families. Other researchers categorize street children according to the strength of family ties; for example, Felsman (1985) identified three different groups of street children in Calí, Colombia: (1) children who were orphaned or abandoned by their families, (2) children who apparently made an "active, willful departure from home" to live on the streets, and (3) those who "actively maintain family ties" (p. 4). Finally, other researchers have used a combination of demographic indicators to categorize children; for example, Martins (1996) identified four different groups of street children in São José, Brazil, based on school attendance, occupation on the streets, and family ties. Although these different classification schemes may make sense in the context of a particular research project, they can make it difficult to draw comparisons across studies.

A related problem is that researchers typically do not establish the reliability of the procedures used to define a child as belonging to any given category. Even broad categories like children *on* or *of* the streets are problematic. Children or adolescents who do not know the whereabouts of their family are very rare in most countries. In our samples, almost every child we have classified as *of* the streets had some contact with kin (a mother, brothers and sisters, uncles or aunts, or other adults they considered "family"). Often these children go home for varying periods of time, becoming children *on* the streets; similarly, children who work on the streets but live at home may periodically leave home and live on the streets for weeks or months. The variability within these two groups regarding frequency of contact with the family, sleeping location, activity during the day, what they do with the money they earn, how many years they attended school, and other characteristics is so large that the distinction between children *of* the streets and children *in* the streets for research or intervention purposes may be meaningless or misleading (Koller and Hutz, 1996).

To allow other researchers to understand the findings and replicate a study, it is imperative that researchers describe their sample with precision and detail. It is not enough to give the age and gender of the participants; the criteria used to categorize the children should be described in sufficient detail to allow other researchers to employ them in their own research. In the long term, perhaps a more appropriate way of classifying street children would be in terms of the risks to which they are exposed (for example, contact with gangs, use of drugs, dropping out of school, and lack of proper parental guidance) and the protective factors available to them (such as attending school, supportive social networks, and access to caring adults). Researchers could then begin to determine how vulnerable children are to developmental risk. Methodologies to evaluate risk are slowly developing, mostly from the research on resilience (Rutter, 1987; Hutz and Koller, 1996), but the assessment of risk factors and protective mechanisms is still difficult and unreliable (Cowan, Cowan, and Schultz, 1996), although some research assessing risk with street children is available (Raffaelli and others, 1995).

**Sampling Issues.** Having decided whom to study and defined the population, the next step is to obtain a study sample. As in all research, street child research must deal with the question of how representative the sample is and whether it is reasonable to generalize from the results of any given study to street children overall. Because street children are not found in fixed settings but instead are dispersed around the street environment, obtaining a truly representative sample is extremely challenging. Researchers can never know how many street children are in other locations that are not covered by the research. And even when researchers work in defined settings, obtaining a random sample is difficult. In our experience (Hutz, Koller, Bandeira, and Forster, 1995), street children rarely refuse to participate in research. In fact, many children approach the researchers and ask to participate; some children even try to be interviewed more than once. Nevertheless, it would be easy for children to walk away without being noticed by the researchers.

There are a number of strategies researchers can use to ensure that their sample is representative. The best strategy is to become familiar with the streets, work with community agencies, and get to know the children and adolescents who will be studied. Using street children as key informants (or even as recruiters) may also increase the chances of obtaining a representative sample. Replication of research in different settings is essential and, in the long run, is the only way to increase the confidence in one's findings.

## Measurement Issues

It is difficult to collect structured data from street children. Researchers who conduct their research in street settings must compete with a number of distractions. In many countries, street children are found in groups, and interviewing them individually is a challenge. Children who are not being interviewed try to listen and participate; bystanders may interrupt to ask what the child has done or to see if the interviewer needs help. In addition, street children learn very fast that to survive on the streets, they must be alert to what goes on around them. Unless danger or the opportunity to make some money is present, they will not focus their attention on anything for more than a few minutes. Thus researchers never have children's attention entirely or for long. Finally, unlike children who live in stable homes and attend school regularly, street children are not used to talking to adults about themselves or paying attention to tasks proposed by adults (Hutz and Koller, 1997; Koller and Hutz, 1996). Despite these challenges, research with street youth has been successfully conducted using a variety of methods, including surveys, observations, and psychological tests.

**Surveys.** Structured interviews or questionnaires have been used as the main (and often only) instrument in research with street youth. This practice has been questioned; for example, Connolly and Ennew (1996) argue that the use of questionnaires that are not constructed from long-term prior observation "effectively invalidates the results of almost all research on street children populations to date" (p. 140). This point may be overstated, as survey research with street children has generated a body of data that shows consistencies across research settings. In multimethod studies, triangulation reveals that survey data are often consistent with data obtained with other methods. However, the need for careful construction of survey instruments based on familiarity with the population to be studied should be emphasized.

It is important that appropriate language be used in the construction of survey protocols. Children may feel ashamed when they do not understand what an adult is saying, and street children are no exception. Rather than ask for clarification, they may give answers that are meaningless or say they have to leave. The interviewer must be alert to nonverbal language—facial expressions, gestures, or changes in the speed of speech—that indicate lack of comprehension or anxiety. Researchers should also take specific characteristics of the participants into account. For example, questions or tasks structured to use recognition instead of recall will usually produce more reliable data. In addition, questions that involve time periods, using expressions such as "last month" or "how many times in the past year," may generate unreliable data since street youth may not have a sense of calendar time. The same question asked a few hours later may bring a different answer. We have found that some children, especially those who do not go to school, have trouble understanding questions about time (Koller and Hutz, 1996). However, researchers have developed innovative methods for studying street children's use of time. For example, Suman Verma has had success using a game to obtain information regarding daily activities from Indian street children (see Verma and Bhan, 1996).

The length of the interview protocol may also affect children's willingness to participate. Many street children in southern Brazil can read and will ask to see the interview protocol. As a result, a researcher with a twenty-page questionnaire may have trouble finding participants. If notes are taken, some children will ask to see them. Therefore, interviewers should be careful not to write down interpretations or comments that they would not want the child to see. Extensive notes, comments, and impressions can be written immediately after the interview, away from the children. In our experience, street children do not mind tape recordings if they trust the interviewer. However, extra time must be allotted to let the children hear themselves on tape, which they enjoy.

During data collection, interviewers must be attentive to the fact that street children's responses are affected by the immediate context and by the perceived consequences of giving the requested information. Obviously, if children believe that the information they are passing on will have no adverse consequences, they will talk more freely and easily. The presence of street adults, gang leaders, pimps, or police officers may also affect a child's willingness to talk.

A question that has generated much debate among researchers concerns how "street wisdom" influences the quality of the data street children provide. Because street children learn that it is to their advantage to tell adults stories that impress, frighten, and elicit pity or approval, some researchers believe that during a research study street children may lie or say whatever they think the researcher wants to hear. In our experience, this tendency can be overcome by a skilled interviewer who detects these occurrences and calls the child's attention to them. This must be done in an empathic way, showing that what the child is trying to do is being understood but what the interviewer really wants to hear is a true story. If done right, this will strengthen the quality of the relationship, and the interviewer will earn some respect. When street children realize that the researcher knows their reality, understands their attitudes, and is indeed paying attention to what they are saying, it becomes possible to collect truthful and reliable data. Although "street wisdom" is sometimes described as an attempt to fool or deceive the researcher, we believe that in most cases it is just an effective way of attracting attention or eliciting desired feelings. In our work, we seldom detect stories that are completely false. To check the reliability of the data, we systematically have two or three interviewers talk to the same children at different times and have typically found that the stories are very consistent.

**Observations and Ethnographic Approaches.** Observation of children on the streets allows researchers to gather information about behaviors in natural settings. Such observations may serve as a preliminary step for future direct approaches or as an independent data source (for example, Raffaelli and others, 1993). To conduct structured observations, researchers must be familiar with the streets and select places where children have a higher probability of displaying the behaviors that are of interest for the research. Researchers must establish observation criteria to increase the reliability of the observations (pilot studies are often necessary). This work is best done by pairs of researchers so that notes can be taken without interrupting the observation. Training is necessary to achieve interrater reliability on coding criteria. No matter who the research participants are, it is difficult to observe them objectively and to list actual behaviors instead of interpretations.

Participant observation methods may also serve as a rich source of information (see Chapter Two). However, because few psychological researchers are trained in ethnographic approaches, informal or unstructured observations may yield unreliable results and should be used with caution.

**Psychological Assessments.** Tests developed to assess motor and cognitive development, intelligence, emotional adjustment, and other indicators of psychological functioning have not been used very frequently in research with street children. The most commonly used have been the Human Figure Drawings, Raven's Progressive Matrices, and the Bender Gestalt test (Aptekar, 1989; Bandeira, Koller, Hutz, and Forster, 1994; Tyler, Tyler, Echeverry, and Zea, 1991). Because of the lack of privacy on the street, researchers who want to use psychological tests must find a place that allows for proper administration of these instruments, such as a shelter or a school. However, if all data are collected with populations from shelters or schools, the results cannot be generalized to street children in general.

Another issue to consider when using psychological tests with street children is that these instruments were not designed for use with impoverished individuals who have little or no formal education. Furthermore, these instruments been not adapted for use with street children, their reliability and validity have not been established, and no norming studies have been conducted. Even when national or regional norms exist, it is very unlikely that such norms would be appropriate for homeless street children in particular. These youngsters have been socialized in a different way, and they use language differently from other children. Researchers should therefore be cautious when using standardized assessments of psychological functioning with street youth.

## How to Approach Street Children

No recipe for becoming a successful street child researcher can be provided. Success in obtaining reliable responses from street children is directly proportional to the researcher's knowledge about and proficiency with the population. The more knowledgeable and proficient the interviewer, the less effort and competency is required from the child (Garbarino and Stott, 1992). Researchers must be prepared to communicate effectively with the children, be empathic, and be capable of listening to whatever is being said without prejudice.

**Selecting and Training Researchers.** The selection of researchers to work on the streets requires a great deal of caution. Many people volunteer for this kind of work because they feel sorry for street children and want to help them. Researchers who hold such feelings often have problems once the real work begins. Depression is the most common consequence, as researchers become overwhelmed by imagining how sad and desperate they themselves would feel if they had to face the adversities of the streets. Well-meaning individuals who do not understand and control their feelings may actually harm the children they wish to help by strengthening the children's feelings of exclusion and making them feel helpless. Unless novice researchers can learn to deal with their emotional response, they are unlikely to perform adequately once data collection begins. At the opposite end of the spectrum are individuals who perceive street children as outcasts or juvenile delinquents, instead of as children who are developing under very harsh circumstances. Researchers who view the children as criminals will not last long in the field; their fear of or disregard for street children will prevent them from working effectively.

A training program for researchers who want to work with street children must address several theoretical and practical issues. Obviously, researchers must be very familiar with the research topics and have basic training in interview techniques before going to the streets. In addition, knowledge about psychological development under adverse circumstances is helpful. Researchers must also be aware of the effects of commonly used drugs and be trained to assess whether a child is fit to be interviewed or tested. Many details that may seem unimportant must be clarified; for example, researchers must learn how to dress, whether to wear jewelry, and how much money they should carry (see, for example, Gunther, 1992).

The most important aspect of the training is to prepare researchers to deal with their feelings toward street children. At our center, this is done in ongoing seminars in which fantasies and fears can be discussed. These seminars start before novice researchers go to the streets and continue throughout the research process. We find that it is after the first experiences in approaching street children that the seminars become effective. It is only after actual contact has been made that a variety of conflicting emotions become real—fear resulting from exposure to the dangers of the street, revulsion caused by the smell of unwashed bodies and drugs, guilt stemming from a desire to reward the children, and impotence over the children's situation. Researchers need help dealing with these mixed and powerful emotions; ongoing supervision is a crucial component for a successful program.

The goal of the training program is to make researchers confident that they can go to the streets and do research. Although groups are usually trained together, the length and amount of training must be tailored for each individual. Some students and psychologists in our training program are ready to start after two or three weeks; others need training for more than six months.

**Establishing a Working Relationship with Street Children.** To collect high-quality data, the researcher must establish a proper working relationship with street children. The character of this relationship will depend in large part on how the researcher approaches the children. Researchers must always be aware that they are dealing with persons from a different world or "culture," even if they were born in the same city. A primary task in cross-cultural communication is to understand how different groups express meaning through their behavior. Researchers must also learn to recognize and deal with status expectations and coping mechanisms employed by different groups. They must also be aware that street children may differ from other children in how they understand, approach, or react to interview questions or research tasks.

When researchers are new in the field and are not known by the street children, the first challenge is to develop trust. In Brazil, street children tend to be very suspicious of adults who approach them. A typical first reaction is to ask for money or just to say that they do not have anything to offer. The first contacts are crucial. If researchers fail to overcome the distrust and suspicion, they will not get useful information or reliable data. The research team needs someone known and trusted by at least some street children. Street educators or people who work for agencies that give assistance to street children can be helpful in the early stages of research.

How children are approached will vary as a function of the kind of street children involved, whether they already know the researchers, and the purpose of the study. If researchers plan to ask personal questions or require information that might jeopardize the study participants' safety, they may need to work with the children until a relationship based on trust is established. Potential participants should be informed about what researchers are trying to accomplish and how the information will be used. We always tell the children and adolescents that we are university professors or students and that our research has academic objectives. We have learned that they understand what that means and that they feel much more comfortable when they know that we are not reporters or police officers.

On a practical note, researchers often neglect to assess how much time the potential research participant has available. In most Brazilian cities, this is especially important if the approach takes place late in the afternoon. At that time, street children who did not make enough money to take home or to pay their adult protectors or who still have not eaten or found a safe place to spend the night will not be willing to participate in a study. Before approaching a street child, the researcher must observe and understand what he or she is doing. Sometimes street children may be too busy to talk to researchers.

**Using Inducements.** It is a common practice for North American researchers to pay study participants or at least give children some reward for participating in a study. We will argue here that this practice is not appropriate in research with street children for both methodological and ethical reasons.

In a typical street research situation, several teams will go out to the streets simultaneously so that most children in a given location or neighborhood can be interviewed at the same time. If inducements (money, clothing, or anything else of value) are distributed, street children will often attempt to be interviewed several times by different teams, in order to receive the inducement each time. They will say anything they think the interviewer wants to hear, as quickly as possible; therefore, the quality of the data will be poor.

Aside from methodological considerations, using inducements with street children may be ethically questionable (Hutz, Koller, Bandeira, and Forster, 1995). Often a street child is hungry or needs money to take home or to buy drugs. Under these circumstances, the use of inducements may coerce the child to participate in the study. If researchers want to ensure that street children participate in the study because they want to, not because they need the money or are hungry, no material inducements should be used. Other forms of assistance may be appropriate; at our center, after data collection is complete, researchers may give the children information or referrals for social services.

Even when no inducements are used, it must be remembered that the opportunity to speak with a trained researcher is by itself rewarding. We have found that even without inducements, street children often try to be interviewed again because they enjoy talking to someone about themselves. They seldom have the experience of meeting an adult who will listen and try to understand what they are saying. Trained researchers are friendly and empathic and do not make value judgments. If children perceive the researcher as an adult who cares and is interested in what they have to say, a positive relationship is established, and the interaction with the interviewer becomes rewarding in itself.

## Ethical Issues

Researchers who work with street children must contend with a number of ethical concerns on top of those common in research with disenfranchised children and adolescents. Two major ethical concerns involve protecting the rights of research participants and ensuring that studies are well designed.

**Protecting Research Participants.** One concern in research with street children involves the impossibility of obtaining true informed consent. It is usually not possible to secure parental consent because finding the parents—if they exist—is very difficult. Researchers can get the participants' assent to participate, but in many countries minors cannot legally give informed consent. Even if youngsters are considered "emancipated minors" because they are living on their own, many children do not have the cognitive skills to understand all the implications and possible consequences of the research (Hurley, 1997).

The problem is compounded by the lack of institutional ethical control of research with human participants in many developing countries. In Brazil, for example, binding ethical guidelines for research were established only recently, and most universities still do not have ethics committees or review boards to evaluate research projects. This situation places a great burden on researchers. In our center, we have dealt with this situation by establishing a mechanism for independent review of research projects. Ad hoc ethics committees can be used to review research projects, but researchers must ascertain that the members of such committees are familiar with research involving street children or, at least, children at social risk. This is important because the assessment of risk in research with street children is a complex issue. In any kind of research, the concept of minimal risk is problematic (Levine, 1986). Often it means that researchers believe that the risks of physical or psychological harm are not greater than those encountered in daily life (Levine, 1991). However, street children actually face large risks in everyday life, including the risk of violent death. Therefore, other criteria are needed for risk assessment. A reasonable solution might be the adoption in research with street children of the same standards employed to define minimal risk for research with low-socioeconomic-status children and adolescents.

**Designing Sound Research.** A second ethical consideration involves the need for ensuring that research studies are as free of methodological limitations as possible. Research conducted with street children is often used to design public policies and intervention programs. However, the reliability and validity of data collected from street children are always doubtful (Aptekar, 1994). The probability that results can be replicated is unknown, even when large effect sizes are found in a specific sample. If the conditions under which data were collected are not taken into account when reporting and evaluating the findings, inappropriate actions may be taken, bad decisions may follow, and harm may be done to the population. Eventually, replication studies or new studies with improved methodologies will detect and correct mistakes and errors; this is a strength of the scientific method. However, when the error is eventually found, it may be too late for the children and adolescents who were affected by ill-designed public policies.

Because of this, research must be very carefully designed, reported, and interpreted. Samples should be described in sufficient detail to make sure that readers know exactly who the participants were. The results must be reported with enough information to allow other researchers to use them for further analysis, including meta-analysis (for example, confidence intervals and sample sizes must be reported). In the absence of replication studies, researchers should treat their results with caution and temper their conclusions. When street children are involved, it may be a good idea to ask what could possibly happen if the results are wrong but decision makers believe they are sound.

## Conclusions

In this chapter, we have identified a number of methodological and ethical challenges inherent in research with street children and attempted to provide suggestions for overcoming them. Many of the methodological issues we raised are researchable and could be systematically investigated. Research with a methodological focus would provide valuable information to street child researchers and could lead to an improvement in the way data are collected and interpreted.

We hope that we have conveyed the message that research with street children raises more ethical concerns than research with middle-class populations. Researchers who want to study street children must develop a familiarity with their language and culture so as to permit collection of valid and reliable data. They should also become familiar with the communities where the children live and know the resources that are available so that they can conduct research that is relevant to the population. Most important, researchers must always keep in mind that when they start studying street children, they will develop a relationship that entails many sometimes daunting responsibilities.

# References

Aptekar, L. "Characteristics of the Street Children of Colombia." *Child Abuse and Neglect,* 1989, *13,* 427–439.

Aptekar, L. "Street Children in·the Developing World: A Review of Their Conditions." *Cross-Cultural Research,* 1994, *28,* 195–224.

Bandeira, D., Koller, S. H., Hutz, C., and Forster, L. "O cotidiano dos meninos de rua de Porto Alegre" [The Daily Life of Street Children in Porto Alegre]. In *Proceedings of the Seventeenth International School Psychology Colloquium.* Campinas, Brazil, 1994.

Barker, G., and Knaul, F. *Exploited Entrepreneurs: Street and Working Children in Developing Countries.* Working Paper no. 1. New York: Childhope USA, 1991.

Campos, R., and others. "Social Networks and Daily Activities of Street Youth in Belo Horizonte, Brazil." *Child Development,* 1994, *65,* 319–330.

Connolly, M., and Ennew, J. "Introduction: Children out of Place." *Childhood,* 1996, *3,* 131–145.

Cowan, P. A., Cowan, C. P., and Schultz, M. S. "Thinking About Risk and Resilience in Families." In E. M. Hetherington and E. A. Blechman (eds.), *Stress, Coping, and Resiliency in Children and Families.* Mahwah, N.J.: Erlbaum, 1996.

Dallape, F. "Urban Children: A Challenge and an Opportunity." *Childhood,* 1996, *3,* 283–294.

Felsman, J. K. *Abandoned Children Reconsidered: Prevention, Social Policy, and the Trouble with Sympathy.* ERIC Document ED268457, 1985.

Garbarino, J., and Stott, F. M. *What Children Can Tell Us: Eliciting, Interpreting, and Evaluating Critical Information from Children.* San Francisco: Jossey-Bass, 1992.

Gunther, H. "Interviewing Street Children in a Brazilian City." *Journal of Social Psychology,* 1992, *132,* 359–367.

Hurley, J. C. "Children's Capacity to Give Truly Informed Assent for Research Participation and Their Understanding of Debriefing." Presentation at the biennial meeting of the Society for Research in Child Development, Washington, D.C., Apr. 1997.

Hutz, C. S., and Koller, S. H. "Resiliência e vulnerabilidade em crianças em situação de risco" [Resilience and Vulnerability in Children at Risk]. *Coletâneas da ANPEPP,* 1996, *1* (12), 79–86.

Hutz, C. S., and Koller, S. H. "Questões sobre o desenvolvimento de crianças em situação de rua" [Issues About the Development of Street Children]. *Estudos de Psicologia,* 1997, *2,* 175–197.

Hutz, C. S., Koller, S. H., Bandeira, D. R., and Forster, L. M. *Researching Street Children: Methodological and Ethical Issues.* ERIC Document PS023280, 1995.

Koller, S. H., and Hutz, C. S. "Meninos E meninas em situação de rua: Dinâmica, diversidade e definição" [Boys and Girls on the Streets: Dynamics, Diversity, and Definition]. *Coletâneas da ANPEPP,* 1996, *1* (12), 11–34.

Levine, R. J. *Ethics and Regulation of Clinical Research.* (2nd ed.) Baltimore: Urban & Schwarzenberg, 1986.

Levine, R. J. "Respect for Children as Research Subjects." In M. Lewis (ed.), *Child and Adolescent Psychiatry: A Comprehensive Textbook.* Baltimore: Williams & Wilkins, 1991.

Martins, R. A. "Censo de crianças e adolescentes em situação de rua em São José do Rio Preto" [A Census of Street Children and Adolescents in São José do Rio Preto]. *Psicologia Reflexão e Crítica,* 1996, *9,* 101–122.

Raffaelli, M., and others. "Sexual Practices and Attitudes of Street Youth in Belo Horizonte, Brazil." *Social Science and Medicine,* 1993, *37,* 661–670.

Raffaelli, M., and others. "HIV-Related Knowledge and Risk Behaviors of Street Youth in Belo Horizonte, Brazil." *AIDS Education and Prevention,* 1995, *7,* 287–297.

Rutter, M. "Psychosocial Resilience and Protective Mechanisms." *American Journal of Orthopsychiatry,* 1987, *57,* 316–331.

Tyler, F. B., Tyler, S. L., Echeverry, J. J., and Zea, M. C. "Making It on the Streets in Bogotá: A Psychosocial Study of Street Youth." *Genetic, Social, and General Psychology Monographs,* 1991, *117,* 395–417.

Verma, S., and Bhan, T. P. "Daily Life Activities in the Physical and Social Milieu of Indian Street Children." Presentation at the Fourteenth Biennial Meeting of the International Society for the Study of Behavioral Development, Quebec, Canada, Aug. 12–16, 1996.

CLAUDIO S. HUTZ *and* SÍLVIA H. KOLLER *are professors in the Department of Psychology of the Federal University of Rio Grande do Sul, Brazil.*

*Efforts to reverse the developmental plight of homeless and working street youth require that their situation be understood from a multilevel public health and human rights perspective.*

# Children at the Margins of Society: Research and Practice

*Felton Earls, Maya Carlson*

What do we need to know to do a better job of protecting children from a life of marginalized existence and exploitative work on the streets of urban centers? Does this knowledge compel policies and actions that result in the recovery of children already exposed and the protection of vulnerable children not yet exposed to such a lamentable life? How well does this volume contribute to that base of knowledge?

This chapter is intended to provide responses to these three questions. We approach these questions from the perspective of public health scientists with a commitment to promoting and protecting the well-being of populations in the widest sense. It is an all too rare occurrence to have knowledge generated from the actual conditions that create grave threats to the survival and well-being of children. Academic researchers have acquired a penchant for positioning themselves at a safe distance from the brunt of bitter reality. In contrast, the authors represented in this volume have placed themselves squarely in the face of the adversities they hope to understand. These chapters, written by human developmentalists, represent a base of research of immediate relevance to public health applications throughout the world.

## A Framework to Guide Health Promotion in Pursuit of Child Well-Being

Public health practitioners and scientists are trained to pursue a variety of strategies and techniques to measure and monitor the extent to which a society achieves a satisfactory and sustainable level of well-being for all its children. This mission to protect and promote the well-being of a population of children requires a statement of purpose and a framework that reflects both the ethical and scientific demands of this task. The framework must also reflect a sensitivity to age and gender, socioeconomic gradients, and racial and ethnic groups within and across societies to ensure that the needs and capacities of all individuals are treated fairly.

Scholars have been reluctant to articulate the full scope of such a design. Yet such a framework is necessary to address the developmental consequences of child exploitation, abuse, and neglect. In positioning themselves to encounter and study children at the margins of society, these authors have all struggled to answer the first of our questions, what we need to understand better about children living and working on the streets. They have variously introduced aspects of history, demography, and economics in an effort to recognize that the conditions under which these children live are driven by forces far removed from the proximal circumstances that condition their daily lives. But no single formula is adopted for placing children in such a vast context, let alone for identifying what aspects of the context one should emphasize for a particular group of children. Our objective is to provide a conceptual framework that will facilitate consistent and long-term progress toward ensuring a high standard of good health and well-being for all children.

In several projects involving street and working children in which we have participated, three elements of this larger framework have emerged (Carlson and Earls, forthcoming; Earls and Eisenberg, 1996). These comprise principles of human rights, health promotion, and multilevel causal analysis. The human rights focus emerges from the very notion of how the definition of childhood is changing and what limits to this definition societies are willing to tolerate. In recent years, the entire concept of childhood has been reconstructed (Hart, 1991). According to the United Nations Convention on the Rights of the Child (UNCRC), children are citizens (Limber and Flekkoy, 1996). The idea that they are simply immature creatures whose needs must be met by parents or other charitably inclined adults is becoming obsolete. As citizens, children have rights that entitle them to the resources required to protect and promote their development. And foremost among those principles is the right to have a family. The children who are the core of this book have as a consequence of their daily experiences this most basic and universal right violated. This is, at once, the most flagrant of abuses and the most difficult one to repair. The journey through the streets of India, Brazil, Kenya, and the United States is stark, yet intensely provocative, because it touches the very base of what it means to be a child.

The principles of health promotion, our second element, have become fundamental in contemporary public health as scientific evidence has accumulated on the environmental supports required for persons to stay healthy or to augment their sense of well-being (Green and Kreuter, 1991). This tradition is expanding beyond the strategies that have characterized the more traditional public health emphasis on disease prevention by fostering concepts of well-being as more than the absence of disease and the quality of life as more than the control of risk factors for specific diseases. This approach applies to children living in disadvantaged or depriving conditions because such circumstances are directly linked to problems such as crime, violence, and sexually transmitted diseases (Earls, Cairns, and Mercy, 1993; Earls and Carlson, 1995; Stiffman and Earls, 1990).

The third element involves specification of a multilevel perspective in which determinants of well-being operate through family, neighborhood, economic, and social structures. Theory development requires that these components be integrated into a coherent system through which both the direction and the strength of causal forces operate. Not only are investigators likely to achieve a more complete understanding of children's developmental and health outcomes with this approach, but they are more likely to contribute to heath promotion efforts to improve the quality of children's lives.

The task of moving from a multilevel theory to the actual implementation of research designs that test the theory constitutes a long-term agenda for the social and behavioral sciences. This formidable objective sits at the core of our study of children's development in a large American city, a study that aims to characterize the multiple influences of neighborhoods, schools, and families on children's behavioral and health outcomes (Earls and Buka, 1997). Although the study was initially focused on capturing the salient risk factors of urban neighborhoods and families, considerable progress is being made in conceptualizing and measuring phenomena of interest in health-promotional terms (Earls and Carlson, 1995; Sampson, Raudenbush, and Earls, 1997). The chapters in this book add critically important insight to studies such as ours through their analysis of both the objective reality and the subjective experience of children in challenging urban contexts.

## Sampling and Recruiting Strategies in Studying Street and Working Children

Encountering children outside the customary contours of family, school, and neighborhood establishes the child development researcher in an unique position. One's attitude about children, research, and the nature of a particular society has to adapt to these appalling circumstances. The preceding chapter prepares one to confront such conditions and the children so captured. Wisely, its authors, Hutz and Koller, underscore the importance of establishing a trusting relationship as a necessary step toward collecting valid data. In our experience, this is so important and so difficult to achieve that it might be given even greater emphasis. It is a topic that deserves space at the top of any research agenda on street and working children.

Hutz and Koller are also savvy in discussing the problems surrounding sampling and efforts to classify the children's predicaments. They assert, "To allow other researchers to understand the findings and replicate a study, it is imperative that researchers describe their sample with precision and detail. It is not enough to give the age and gender of the participants; the criteria used to categorize the children should be described in sufficient detail to allow other researchers to employ them in their own research. In the long term, perhaps a more appropriate way of classifying street children would be in terms of the risks to which they are exposed . . . and the protective factors available to them." This is a most important statement to make in an area of investigation that remains daunting and relatively uncommon in child development research. What makes this so essential is that the commonalities among street and working children around the world are more striking than the contrasts. The feasibility and the desirability for replication and extending work from one area of the world to another are quite sound. Such replications not only provide a sturdier body of knowledge but are critically important in substantiating the claims made in the UNCRC.

Chapters One and Two, on children in India and Brazil, respectively, provide ample evidence of the need for nuanced research. These studies combine ethnographic and ecological methods to provide complex and intimate depictions of the relationships and difficulties children experience on a daily basis and the strategies they adopt to survive. We are particularly impressed by Suman Verma's reference in Chapter One to the work of Barker and Wright (1955; see also Barker and Wright, 1949) on behavioral settings, since their emphasis on understanding behavior in context has been undermined in much of contemporary psychology.

The descriptions provided in these two chapters remind one of urban ecologies frequented by street and working children in films such as *Salaam Bombay, Pixote, Streetwise,* and Buñuel's splendid classic, *Los Olvidados.* It becomes easy to understand how these children have lost faith in humanity. They are wary of adult authority in general and fear the police in particular. Autonomy has become the precious residual of not having the protection of a family, school, or village, and they should not be expected to give it up readily. They are easy prey for drugs, and after some number of months in the urban wilderness, the probability increases that they will be sexually exploited.

If children living on the streets happen to reside in relatively benign contexts where the AIDS virus, crack cocaine, or guns have not penetrated their world, it may only be a matter of time, given global dynamics, before these dangers surface. We witnessed this happening while visiting shelters for street children in Cape Town, Durban, and Johannesburg, South Africa. This reality was cast in a particular kind of irony since the society was emerging from decades of oppressive government treatment. The difficult question had to be asked: Could a liberated society protect its children any better than the oppressive one had? Thus researchers are forced to understand and deal with the fact that research on marginalized children involves a dynamic system in which economic and political factors play a dominant role.

Jacqueline Smollar, in Chapter Four, underscores how the definition of marginalized youth changes as one enters the highly developed setting of a metropolitan area in the United States. The terms *runaways* and *throwaways* have been adopted to reflect the putative reasons why children are found on

the streets. The historical perspective demonstrates that the population com-
position of homeless youth has changed during the twentieth century. Since
poverty has been increasing over the past two decades for families with children, Smollar is correct in pointing out that this may once again become a
major cause of youth homelessness.

## Some Conceptual Issues Related to Studying Street and Working Children

A matter germane to research with children in adverse situations concerns the
concept of resilience. Here we conceive of resilience as the capacity to recover
from a setback. Our view does not readily differentiate this construct as an
innate capacity of the individual from the provision of environmental supports and opportunities. We have found the issue conceptually difficult to
apply in work with disadvantaged children generally and street children
specifically. In large part this is because the concept is most readily applied to
children experiencing acutely stressful conditions. When children and their
families must adapt to conditions of persistent stress, when they are faced
with an ever-present sense of insecurity, and when the future is largely outside the bounds of their sense of efficacy, resilience becomes not an expectable
but an extraordinary achievement.

As the chapters in this book indicate, children spending appreciable time
on the street must adapt to what are often unpredictable and threatening circumstances. There are skills involved in being able to manage this state of
affairs over time, but to think that many children can survive without serious
harm to their capacity to trust others, to cherish intimacy and privacy, and to
plan and forecast their lives over long horizons is not supported through available knowledge. The most pressing problem is how to embrace such children
and sustain a supportive relationship long enough to assist them in making the
transition from the margins of society to more constructive roles and responsibilities. For that to be achieved, more systematic analysis of the services available to street and working children must be obtained.

None of the chapters focused extensively on the role that cultural and
racial or ethnic factors might assume in the prevalence, location, or serious-
ness of homelessness. Yet in each of the societies included in this volume, such
factors represent a prominent feature. When we first encountered Brazilian
street children, we were surprised to find that the majority of these children,
even in the south, were of African heritage. In fact, there appeared to be a
noticeable association between skin color (for which there are many fine gra-
dations in Brazilian society) and occupational prestige. It was not race but
poverty that explained the high proportion of black youth on the streets of Rio
de Janeiro and São Paulo. Nonetheless, the issue as to why Afro-Brazilians were
less prosperous than Brazilians of European background was not openly discussed. In U.S. cities, health services and shelters accessible to street youth
have significant numbers of white youths, and these youths have often been

exposed to highly dysfunctional families (Earls, Robins, Stiffman, and Powell, 1989; Stiffman and Earls, 1990). This should not imply that there is a lower proportion of African-American youths from dysfunctional homes; rather, attitudes conditioned by racial and class status favor greater proportions of white youth using these publicly available services because black and economically disadvantaged youth perceive themselves as more excluded from all aspects of American society.

The way in which gender influences the street child phenomenon in Nairobi, Kenya, is elaborated in Chapter Three, by Aptekar and Ciano-Federoff. That girls fare worse than boys is revealed by their poorer psychological test performance and their more pathological behavior as uncovered in ethnographic accounts. From a public health perspective, however, the most important finding of the authors' analyses was the revelation that of the two major slum areas in Nairobi, one produces the overwhelming majority of street girls. Although some possible reasons for this are hinted at, the difference between these two areas should become the focus of intensive investigation itself. The fact that girls leave home for the streets at a later age than boys might be taken as a relatively favorable factor, yet it does not appear to be so. One generally assumes that the earlier the entry to street existence and the longer one remains in this predicament, the worse the developmental outcome. Nevertheless, the hypotheses generated from this ethnographic study are that girls experience more severe family rejection than boys do and that this kind of abuse or neglect begins in the home environment and may even be tolerated by the larger social setting in which the family is situated. In contrast to boys, who may be expected to work on the streets, family rejection appears to be the major reason why girls are on the street. Although the question of income generation was not mentioned, the assumption is that males generate more money than females. In other societies—Thailand, for example—income from female prostitution may exceed that earned by males of a similar age and background. An open question is the extent to which parental acceptance or rejection is influenced by the level of income that flows back into the family unit.

Another concern that occupies much of our orientation to work with street and working children regards physical and mental health status. Given their exposures to infections, road accidents, violence, and drugs, not to mention the noise, pollution, and blight of urban areas they inhabit, it is difficult to draw a picture of these children without awareness of how their minds and bodies adapt to and cope with these adversities. For example, a health inquiry would examine for scars and other evidence of injuries, inspect the child's mouth and teeth, inquire about lead exposure, ask if problems with reading exist (even if they are not in school), estimate both the stage and velocity of puberty, ask about sleep patterns, and ascertain if symptoms of wheezing are present. There are relatively few accounts of studies that systematically gather this kind of information about the health of street and working children (Pinto and others, 1994; Porto and others, 1994; Raffaelli and others, 1993; Wright, Kaminsky, and Wittig, 1993). Recently, we began exploring the measurement

of the stress hormone cortisol to examine the consequences of social deprivation and exposure to highly traumatic events in similar populations (Goenjian
and others, 1996; Carlson and Earls, 1997, forthcoming). The goal of this
research is to increase insight into how behavioral and emotional responses to
psychosocial events are regulated by physiological systems. From this perspective, biological processes are viewed as outcomes, not determinants of
behavior. Application of this method to work with street and working children
is feasible, yet it is important to emphasize that such physiological data can
only be interpreted in the context of a child's general health. The point we wish
to make here is the utility of integrating assessments of psychological and physical growth and development into more coherent and holistic approaches.

## Supporting Street Children While Changing the Conditions That Produce Them

Commonalities are observable across settings in the operation of shelters for
street children. Whether in Cape Town, São Paulo, Mexico City, or New
York, street workers who could not know one another, let alone others' care-
taking philosophies, appreciate that it takes months to secure the trust of a
child who has lived on the streets. As these helpers supervise such children,
they learn to expect and anticipate setbacks. Indeed, months of progress can
be undone by a sudden eruption of antisocial behavior. Just as a parent does
not give up on a child who makes mistakes, exhibits poor judgment, or lies,
it is paramount that these workers demonstrate unflinching commitment to
these children. This is hardly straightforward. Few workers are trained to
deal with the exigencies met in dealing the material circumstances and
lifestyles of children living on the street. To add to the burden, inadequate
programmatic funding, low salaries, and an undeniable level of danger can
undermine the strong sense of justice that often motivates individuals into
this work. None of the chapters pursue aspects such as this, but they are crucial to a society's having any chance of rehabilitating these children.

Many societies around the world, developed and developing, are making
efforts to protect, educate, and rehabilitate street and working children. International organizations such as UNICEF and Save the Children are the vanguard
of this movement, and the UNCRC has been a compelling force responsible for
initiating and sustaining these efforts where they exist. But we do want to
emphasize that insufficient importance has been directed to training field-
workers, both in the pursuit of research and in the rendering of human services.
In fact, it seems inadvisable for an individual or group to engage in services only
to children already thoroughly ensconced in life on the streets.

The issue of how to train and engage oneself in a range of supportive,
therapeutic, and preventive activities triggers a predictable reaction in a person committed to public health principles and practices. Remember, we say to
ourselves when working with street and working children, that we are far
downstream. If our ultimate aim is to promote well-being, then how do we

mobilize energy and resources to rescue some children while at the same time creating conditions to reduce the numbers who enter this predicament?

Conceptually, we accomplish a promotional and palliative approach to children's health through a dual process. First, we place populations of marginalized children within a multilevel framework for causal analysis. From India to Brazil to Kenya, the particular factors that enter this model differ according to local circumstances, but the broad categories of national and local economy, government policy, cultural beliefs and values, and structure and functioning of communities and families need to be conceptualized within a single framework. This kind of complex analysis helps one draw together the plight of a single child and the much larger forces that pushed or pulled this child into his or her current predicament. In this regard, the authors of Chapter Two show how the situation of Brazilian street children is related to the historical and political contexts of that society. Agencies responding to the immediate needs of street and working children should not only have the big picture clearly in view but should find ways to work upstream and downstream at the same time.

The second strategy involves adopting a code of ethics conditioned by respect for the dignity of all children. This is no hollow statement. To act ethically toward children who are regularly exploited requires a special kind of preparation and conscientiousness. In teaching students in public health and medicine, we place much emphasis on getting them to understand the subjective experiences of children living on the streets (Earls, 1996; Earls and Carlson, 1996). Role playing, discourse sessions, and critically reviewing novels and films on street children, such as those mentioned earlier, are some techniques we employ to deepen understanding and increase sensitivity toward these children's lives. An excellent example of an ethical dilemma faced by many of our students concerns their reaction to displays of tough love, as described in Chapter Two, in some of the religiously supervised shelters. These authors' description resonates with much that we have also witnessed in visiting shelters in many different places.

The UNCRC, though organized and circulated as a legal document, embodies a set of underlying principles that constitute a code of ethics useful for groups and individuals conducting research or providing services to children in seriously threatening circumstances. The convention represents a set of nonnegotiable claims about the need to protect children from abuse and neglect, ensure them access to the provisions required for healthy development, and promote their genuine participation in society. These claims convey both ethical and scientific knowledge, but they are articulated more in the context of international law than as universal ethical principles. Child care workers need to accept a code of ethics to govern their own conduct and guide their understanding of the difficult responsibilities they carry. But ethics without science is as incomplete as science without ethics. We know a great deal about what constitutes children's healthy development, and this must inform our work with them. The way, then, to judge institutional responses is to ask to what extent they are consistent with both scientific knowledge and the ethical framework suggested by the UNCRC. All else should fall into place once this criterion is met.

## A Framework to Guide Research and Practice

Let us now return to the three questions with which we began this chapter: What do we know that might point the way toward solutions, how compelling is this knowledge, and to what extent has this volume made a significant advance to reach this goal? What we have learned is that the forces driving children into the streets are related to the economic plight of families, conflict and turmoil within families, and the freedom of young people to express an unconventional lifestyle. The conditions vary across societies and across historical periods. It seems safe to say that proportionately, poverty pushes many more children into street labor than are pulled into these contexts by the pursuit of freedom. Not surprisingly, we have also learned that the developmental costs are significant and that they may be costlier for girls than for boys in some settings. This information is provocative because it exposes a set of circumstances that no society should tolerate. But is the evidence compelling enough to motivate governments and citizens to act decisively to reverse the tide? Probably not.

In studying street children, it is not enough just to be aware of the dynamic political, economic, and social factors that characterize a given society. Social scientists must seek ways to integrate these features into their research design and into the theories and frameworks they use to interpret their findings. All of the authors struggle with this in some way. We were confronted with this in conducting research on abandoned and institutionalized infants in Romania (Carlson and Earls, 1997). Despite the fall of a national government that had promulgated a variety of pronatalist policies and the newly arrived availability of contraceptive medications and abortion, the admission rate to institutions remained high. It was as if families, health workers, and the society at large had become conditioned to accepting the abandonment of babies. Without achieving some way of making sense of this phenomenon, it would be impossible to know if the research we were conducting was helping or hindering this situation. Fortunately, we were able to gain sufficient insight through consultation with a number of local NGOs and then carefully explicate our research so that it was consistent with the UNCRC (which Romania has ratified) and helpful to authorities in that country who sought to reduce child abandonment and eliminate the institutions that had been created in the previous era.

The global trend toward urbanization indicates that without a concerted effort to curb the growth of cities and make them habitable environments, the number of squatter families and slum dwellers will continue to swell beyond anything imaginable. The world's economy is rapidly advancing to a two-tiered system of managers and service providers. Estimates are that a relatively small proportion of a population might be able to fulfill the management functions of running a technologically based economy, leaving the vast majority for highly expendable service sector jobs. Not only are disparities of income and wealth increasing in this new world order, but income volatility is also becoming more common. In this flux, a certain proportion of people, especially children, will be perceived as redundant or dispensable.

In contrast to the certainty of these antihuman forms of economic growth and social organization is a dawning awareness that the most important indicator of wealth is the well-being of individuals. Of increasing importance in this regard is the Human Development Index, a metric used to measure well-being of citizens introduced by the United Nations Development Program (1990). It is in the context of the rise of the human rights agenda and a nascent appreciation among economists that both communism and capitalism have failed to promote human development for the great majority of people in the world that the UNCRC stands out (along with several other international manifestos) as yet another sign of progress.

So we are living in a world where we can be both pessimistic that growth is out of control and optimistic that articulation of rights and the admitted failure of our two leading economic motifs provides just the climate for radical change needed to place human development front and center on the world's agenda.

At the end of the twentieth century, one can wonder if the degree of progress in health and education accomplished in this century can be sustained into the next. The chance that this can happen is based on the degree to which we are prepared to monitor the well-being of children as methodically as we have documented the mortality of children. But to accomplish this we need better indicators of good health and well-being. The authors of the Human Development Index have included rates of literacy and educational levels as crude and indirect indicators of well-being. But there should be more directly measured variables to reflect children's mental and physical health and social relations. This is why we need to be armed with precise and accurate information about children at the margins of society. Accurate counts of their numbers, clear depictions of their lives, and valid estimates of the income they earn are indispensable elements with which to construct pictures of their mental lives and physical conditions. Academics have an important role to play in providing theory and methods to collect high-quality data. It is essential that this be done with a degree of conceptual and methodological uniformity to permit comparisons and contrasts across cultural and national groups. Ethnographic and descriptive approaches represent an important step toward this goal, but they should be combined with larger-scale surveys that document the growth parameters, health status, and psychosocial development of these children.

UNICEF and several other international organizations already do a creditable job of integrating detailed case description and statistical data, but their research is confined to data that are collected for administrative rather than scientific reasons. The development of innovative and probing methods as they relate to consequential issues in the growth and development of street, working, and homeless children represents a unique contribution made by the contributors to this volume. We need to document and know as much about the lives of these children as we possibly can, for without serious and sustained effort to prevent this compromised existence for children, we will not be able to carry out the revolution promised in the UNCRC. We will continue to permit societies that are absorbed with economic development to persist in producing the conditions that generate large numbers of marginalized children.

This volume is steeped in a tradition that has been minimized in modern psychology: one marked particularly by the theoretical contributions of Kurt Lewin, Roger Barker, and Urie Bronfenbrenner. It is a tradition that is at last reemerging in developmental psychology. As research in this area reconnects to real-life settings, opportunities arise to understand children in ways that are different and, we hope, more valid than what can be achieved in laboratory settings. This exposure of developmental psychology to the world also compels the field to combine efforts with other disciplines and professions that are at work on improving the human condition—public health, sociology, urban planning, pediatrics, education, and international law are areas that come most readily to mind. Just as the international child rights movement has been propelled by a concern with the plight of street and working children, the field of developmental psychology stands to have its relevance and integrity as a field advanced by the theme addressed and knowledge accumulated in this text.

# References

Barker, R. G., and Wright, H. F. "Psychological Ecology and the Problem of Psychosocial Development." *Child Development,* 1949, *20,* 131–143.

Barker, R. G., and Wright, H. F. *Midwest and Its Children.* New York: HarperCollins, 1955.

Carlson, M., and Earls, F. "Psychological and Neuroendocrinological Sequelae of Early Social Deprivation in Institutionalized Children in Romania." *Integrative Neurobiology of Affiliation, Annals New York Academy of Science,* 1997, *807,* 419–428.

Carlson, M., and Earls, F. "Social Ecology and the Development of Stress Regulation." In L. R. Bergman, R. B. Cairns, L. Nilsson, and L. Nystedt (eds.), *Developmental Science and the Holistic Approach.* Mahwah, N.J.: Erlbaum, forthcoming.

Earls, F. Review of *The Urban Child in Distress: Global Predicaments and Innovative Strategies,* ed. C. Blanc and others. *Childhood,* 1996, *3,* 121–125.

Earls, F., and Buka, S. L. *Project on Human Development in Chicago Neighborhoods: Technical Report.* Rockville, Md.: National Institute of Justice, 1997.

Earls, F., Cairns, R., and Mercy, J. "The Control of Violence and the Promotion of Nonviolence in Adolescents." In S. Millstein, A. Petersen, and E. Nightingale (eds.), *Promoting the Health of Adolescents.* New York: Oxford University Press, 1993.

Earls, F., and Carlson, M. "Promoting Human Capability as an Alternative to Early Crime Prevention." In R. V. Clarke, J. McCord, and P. O. Wikstrom (eds.), *Integrating Crime Prevention Strategies: Propensity and Opportunity.* Stockholm, Sweden: National Council for Crime Prevention, 1995.

Earls, F., and Carlson, M. "The Urban Child in Global Perspective." Course syllabus, Harvard School of Public Health, 1996.

Earls, F., and Eisenberg, L. "International Perspectives in Child Psychiatry." In M. D. Lewis (ed.), *Child and Adolescent Psychiatry: A Comprehensive Textbook.* Baltimore: Williams & Wilkins, 1996.

Earls, F., Robins, L. N., Stiffman, A. R., and Powell, J. "Comprehensive Health Care for High-Risk Adolescents." *American Journal of Public Health,* 1989, *79,* 999–1005.

Goenjian, A. K., and others. "Basal Cortisol, Dexamethasone Suppression of Cortisol, and MHPG in Adolescents After the 1988 Earthquake in Armenia." *American Journal of Psychiatry,* 1996, *153,* 929–934.

Green, L. W., and Kreuter, M. W. *Health Promotion Planning: An Educational and Environmental Approach.* (2nd ed.) Toronto: Mayfield, 1991.

Hart, S. N. "From Property to Person Status: Historical Perspective on Children's Rights." *American Psychologist,* 1991, *46,* 53–59.

Limber, S. P., and Flekkoy, M. G. "The U.N. Convention on the Rights of the Child: Its Relevance for Social Scientists." *Social Policy Report,* 1996, *9*(2), 1–15.

Pinto, J. A., and others. "HIV Risk Behavior and Medical Status of Underprivileged Youths in Belo Horizonte, Brazil." *Journal of Adolescent Health,* 1994, *15,* 179–185.

Porto, S.O.B., and others. "Prevalence and Risk Factors for HBV Infection Among Street Youth in Central Brazil." *Journal of Adolescent Health,* 1994, *15,* 577–581.

Raffaelli, M., and others. "Sexual Practices and Attitudes of Street Youth in Belo Horizonte, Brazil." *Social Science and Medicine,* 1993, *37,* 661–670.

Sampson, R. J., Raudenbush, S. W., and Earls, F. "Neighborhoods and Violent Crime: A Multilevel Study of Collective Efficacy." *Science,* 1997, *277,* 918–924.

Stiffman, A. R., and Earls, F. "Behavioral Risks for Human Immunodeficiency Virus Syndrome in Adolescent Medical Patients." *Pediatrics,* 1990, *85,* 303–310.

United Nations Development Program. "Defining and Measuring Human Development." *Human Development Report,* 1990, pp. 9–16.

Wright, J. D., Kaminsky, D., and Wittig, M. "Health and Social Conditions of Street Children in Honduras." *American Journal Diseases of Children,* 1993, *147,* 279–283.

FELTON EARLS *is professor of human behavior and development at the Harvard School of Public Health and professor of child psychiatry at Harvard University, where he is principal investigator of the Project on Human Development in Chicago Neighborhoods.*

MAYA CARLSON *is associate professor of neurobiology in psychiatry at Harvard Medical School, where she directs the Program on Child Rights and Development.*

# INDEX

United States, homeless youth in (*continued*)
developmental issues of, 51–55; family
dysfunction as causative factor for, 2, 49,
50, 53–54, 55, 76; historical overview of,
48–50, 74–75; personality and behavioral problems of, 50–51; from poor
immigrant families, 48; prevalence of,
47; racial demographics of, 75–76; runaway, 48–49; social policy and service
needs of, 55; study of, 3–4, 47–55
U.S. Congress, 48–49
U.S. National Science Foundation, 36
U.S. Senate, 49, 57
Urban Basic Services for the Poor, 16
Urbanization: and exploitation of child
labor, 7; global trend toward, 79–80;
and prevalence of working street youth
in Brazil, 21; and prevalence of working
street youth in India, 7–8

Varma, A. P., 8, 18
Verma, S., 3, 5, 8, 9, 10, 12, 13, 14, 17,
18, 62, 70, 74

Victims, Kenyan street girls as, 42–43
Vij, R., 13, 18

Wainaina, J., 35, 36, 46
Walsh, G. W., 50, 57
Weiner, M., 7, 18
Well-being, framework for, 71–73,
79–81
Werner, E. E., 52, 57
Whitbeck, L. B., 51, 57
Williams, R., 47, 57
Wittig, M., 76, 82
Working street youth, in India, 5–18, 33.
*See also* India, working street youth in;
Street youth
Wright, H. F., 9, 17, 74, 81
Wright, J. D., 76, 82

Young, R., 50, 57
Younnis, J., 49, 53, 57

Zea, M. C., 64, 70

# Back Issue/Subscription Order Form

Copy or detach and send to:
**Jossey-Bass Inc., Publishers, 350 Sansome Street, San Francisco CA 94104-1342**

Call or fax toll free!
**Phone 888-378-2537 6AM-5PM PST; Fax 800-605-2665**

Back issues:    Please send me the following issues at $25 each.
(Important: please include series initials and issue number, such as CD82.)

1. CD _____

_____

_____

$ _____ Total for single issues

$ _____ Shipping charges (for single issues *only;* subscriptions are exempt from shipping charges): Up to $30, add $5$^{50}$ • $30$^{01}$–$50, add $6$^{50}$ $50$^{01}$–$75, add $7$^{50}$ • $75$^{01}$–$100, add $9 • $100$^{01}$–$150, add $10 Over $150, call for shipping charge.

Subscriptions    Please ❏ start    ❏ renew my subscription to *New Directions for Child and Adolescent Development* for the year 19\_\_\_ at the following rate:

     ❏ Individual $67      ❏ Institutional $115

**NOTE:** Subscriptions are quarterly, and are for the calendar year only. Subscriptions begin with the spring issue of the year indicated above. For shipping outside the U.S., please add $25.

$ _____ Total single issues and subscriptions (CA, IN, NJ, NY and DC residents, add sales tax for single issues. NY and DC residents must include shipping charges when calculating sales tax. NY and Canadian residents only, add sales tax for subscriptions.)

❏ Payment enclosed (U.S. check or money order only)

❏ VISA, MC, AmEx, Discover Card #_____ Exp. date_____

Signature _____ Day phone _____

❏ Bill me (U.S. institutional orders only. Purchase order required.)

Purchase order #_____

Name _____

Address _____

_____

_____

Phone_____ E-mail _____

For more information about Jossey-Bass Publishers, visit our Web site at:
www.josseybass.com      **PRIORITY CODE = ND1**